◁ **W9-DCP-158**

What does "awakening", in the final analysis, actually mean?

"Awakening" means that total disappearance of all phenomenal problems, resulting in a perpetual feeling of total freedom from all worries. It is a feeling of lightness, of floating in the air, untouched by the impurity - and confusion - of the split mind. It is as if the very root of all problems has been demolished, as if the Hydra has been fatally pierced in the heart to prevent the heads from growing again and again.

CHAPTER 5

****

(Seekers) don't realize that all methods and techniques are utterly useless unless they give up the illusion that they themselves are autonomous entities, with volition and choice, working towards a goal.

CHAPTER 9

****

There is no practicer and nothing to practice - no seeker and nothing to seek. Deep apprehension of this is illumination.

CHAPTER 20

****

...the presence of a seeker entity inevitably prevents enlightenment - there is no difference between ignorance and enlightenment as long as there is a conceptual entity to experience either condition.

CHAPTER 20

All rights reserved. No part of this book may be reproduced or transmitted in any form or by any means, electronic or mechanical, including photocopying, recording, or by any information storage and retreival system without written permission from the author or his agents, except for the inclusion of brief quotations in a review.

Copyright © 1988 by

Ramesh S. Balsekar

First Published in United States Of America by

ADVAITA PRESS

P.O. Box 3479

Redondo Beach, California 90277

Designed by: Wayne Liquorman

Cover Art: Rifka Hirsch

Cover Design: Arthur J. Hendrickson

Library of Congress Catalog Card Number: 88-71633

ISBN 0-929448-07-3

EXPERIENCING THE TEACHING

by

RAMESH S. BALSEKAR

ADVAITA PRESS

-LOS ANGELES-

Contents

PREFACE vii

INTRODUCTION ix

CHAPTER 1   SOME BASIC FACETS
            OF THE TEACHING 14

CHAPTER 2   THE DO-ER...26

CHAPTER 3   THINKING--A PERNICIOUS HABIT 29

CHAPTER 4   ENLIGHTENMENT - LIBERATION -
            REALIZATION..34

CHAPTER 5   DREAMING AND AWAKENING 43

CHAPTER 6   "REBIRTH" CONSIDERED.....................49

CHAPTER 7   THE INHERENT IDENTITY 53

CHAPTER 8   THE WHOLE TROUBLE 59

CHAPTER 9   WHO - WHERE - WHEN? 61

CHAPTER 10 WHAT HE THINKS OF ME 65

CHAPTER 11 WHO IS THE PERCEIVER
            WHO PERCEIVES?....................................70

CHAPTER 12 TRUE PERCEIVING 74

CHAPTER 13 THE ESSENCE OF UNDERSTANDING 78

CHAPTER 14 IDENTIFICATION AND
            DISIDENTIFICATION 83

CHAPTER 15   THE PERPETUAL PROBLEM 87

CHAPTER 16   REVERSING INTO THE FUTURE 90

CHAPTER 17   I AM THE PAIN..95

CHAPTER 18   VOLITIONAL EFFORT 99

CHAPTER 19   WHAT WE ARE 105

CHAPTER 20   "BONDAGE AND FREEDOM" -
              SIMPLIFIED 108

CHAPTER 21   SPEAKING OF GOD. 116

CHAPTER 22   OBJECTIVE ABSENCE IS
              SUBJECTIVE PRESENCE 121

CHAPTER 23   UNEXTENDED, YOU ARE HOME 130

CHAPTER 24   THE BEGINNING AND THE END 133

GLOSSARY 137

• PREFACE

Nisargadatta Maharaj had an apparently hearty dislike of professional writers on metaphysics. This was probably based on the well-established premise that those who know do not speak and those who speak do not know. Maharaj himself spoke from experience and repeatedly reminded his listeners of the utter futility of listening to him as one individual entity to another. He said that when he spoke, it was consciousness speaking to consciousness.

Soon after the writing for *Pointers From Nisargadatta Maharaj*[1] began to appear spontaneously, when this fact was conveyed to Maharaj, he seemed not to have been surprised. He said that such inspired writing was called *prasadic*, which could be loosely translated as "a gift from nature or *nisarga*". It is essential to understand that this gift is not made for the benefit of the nominal author but as a gift to those who were in need of it. Such spontaneous writing has continued through *Experience of Immortality* [2]and *Explorations Into The Eternal*[3], and now *Experiencing The Teaching*. It would almost seem that the circle is now complete with this fourth segment. My friend Soumitra Mullarpattan had once expressed to me, after the second book was published, his hope that a

1   Ramesh S. Balsekar, *Pointers From Nisargadatta
     Maharaj* (Bombay: Chetana, 1982)
2   Ramesh S. Balsekar, *Experience Of Immortality*
     (Bombay: Chetana, 1984)
3   Ramesh S. Balsekar, *Explorations Into The Eternal*
     (Bombay: Chetana, 1987)

book would emerge that was based on my own experience of the deeper aspects of Maharaj's Teaching. It would seem that this brief volume is the objectification of that hope.

The essential point in Maharaj's dislike of professional writing on metaphysics was that such writing would be conditioned and limited by the dialectical approach, requiring proof of experiment by anybody at any time. Such an author would be writing on metaphysical matters necessarily from the viewpoint of a bound, identified and supposedly autonomous entity, one who has apparently fully accepted the notion that he is what he appears to be. He would be writing from the viewpoint of an Arjuna and not from that of a Lord Krishna. Such writing from a position of ignorance would not bear the stamp of authority, but could quite easily, because of the relativity of language, seriously mislead the fellow-prisoners. Any expression from behind prison bars can only further delude the already deluded, the delusion being that there are bars and that there is some one behind them.

I have already said elsewhere that there is writing but no author. Perhaps I should add that it is when the reader feels there is reading but no reader, that writing and reading would merge to produce apperception of the kind that never needs a comprehender.

• INTRODUCTION

Before dealing with the question of what precisely *Experiencing The Teaching* is meant to convey, it would be necessary to have an overview of the basics of Nisargadatta Maharaj's Teaching. This may give the reader a clearer idea of the gateless gate at the end of the conceptual pathless path. In order to do this we shall, at this juncture, ignore the side-roads, the by-lanes, and foot-ways and just stick to the highway, though it is necessary to explore the various routes branching off the main road in order to know the whole area thoroughly. Such a study in depth of various aspects of the essence of the Nisargadatta Teaching is provided by the contents of the book itself.

In this introduction let us make an effort to enumerate the precise basics of the Teaching. Perhaps the most attractive feature of the presentation of the Teaching, particularly for the westerners, was the fact that Maharaj scrupulously avoided the use of the spiritual jargon, and indeed rarely referred to the scriptures. He limited his talks to the seeker, the seeker's relationship with other sentient beings, the phenomenal manifestation and its source (Noumenon).

(1) *Noumenon* - pure subjectivity - is not aware of its existence. Such awareness of its existence comes about only with the arising of consciousness - I am. This spontaneous arising of consciousness (because that is its nature, as Maharaj said), brings about the sense of presence, of existence. Simultaneously, it causes the arising of the phenomenal manifestation in consciousness, together with a sense of duality. The Wholeness gets split into the duality of a (pseudo) subject and observed object - each phenomenal object assumes subjectivity as a "me" concerning all other ob-

jects as "others". The objectivization of this duality requires the creation of the twin concepts of "space" and "time": "space" in which the volume of objects could be extended, and "time" in which the phenomenal images extended in space could be perceived, cognized and measured in terms of the duration of existence.

(2) The human beings and all other sentient beings are as much an integral part of the total phenomenal manifestation as any other phenomena. They arise with the arising of the phenomenal universe. As objective phenomena, there is no apparent difference between animate and inanimate objects. But subjectively, it is sentience which is responsible for enabling the sentient beings to perceive. Sentience, as such, is an aspect of consciousness in which the manifestation *occurs*, but it has nothing to do with the *arising* of the manifestation. Thus, although sentience enables human beings to perceive other objects, and intellect enables them to discriminate, they are in no way different from all the other phenomena.

(3) The conceptual bondage arises only because each human phenomenon assumes himself to be an independent entity. As such he considers himself subject to the bonds of space-time as something tangible and extraneous to his own existence.

(4) Noumenality and phenomenality are identical in the sense that noumenality is immanent in phenomenality. Phenomenality has no nature of its own other than noumenality. Noumenality must, at the same time, transcend phenomenality because noumenality is all there is. Phenomenality is merely the objective aspect of noumenality.

It is the identification of noumenality with each separate phenomenon, thus producing a pseudo-subject out of what is merely the operational element in a phenomenal object that produces the phantom of an autonomous individual, the ego, which considers itself to be in conceptual bondage.

The phenomenal functioning as such is quite impersonal, and the illusory entity is wholly unnecessary therein, its place being merely that of an apparatus or mechanism. The impersonal functioning comports impersonal experiencing of both pain and pleasure, and it is only when this experience is interpreted by the pseudo-subject as the experiencer experiencing the experience in duration, that the experienc*ing* loses its intemporal, impersonal element of functioning and assumes the duality of objectivization as subject/object.

(5) What-we-are, as noumenon, is intemporal, infinite, imperceptible being. What-we-appear-to-be as phenomena, is temporal, finite, sensorially perceptible separate objects. Truly, we are illusory figments in consciousness. The fact that we, as separate, illusory entities, absurdly expect to be able to transform ourselves into enlightened beings, shows the extent of the conditioning to which we have been subjected. How can a phenomenon, a mere appearance, perfect itself? Only dis-identification with the supposed entity can bring about the transformation.

(6) It would seem that the mechanism of living is based on the belief that everything that happens in life is the result of acts of volition by the concerned phenomenal objects, the sentient beings. But this would be an incorrect belief because it can be clearly seen that human beings *react* to an outside stimulus rather than act volitionally. Their living is primarily a sequence of reflexes that leaves hardly any room for what might be considered as acts of will or volition. Their way of life is very much conditioned by instinct, habit, propaganda and the latest "fashion". More fundamentally, the fact is that volition is nothing more than an illusory inference, a mere demonstration, a futile gesture by an energized "me-concept". Apart from the psychosomatic mechanism, there is just no entity to exercise volition. All there is, is the impersonal functioning and the inexorable chain of causation.

(7) In the absence of an entity (redundant in the absence of volition), who is there to exercise the illusory volition and who is there to experience the results of it? Who is there to be bound and who is there to be liberated?

The deepest possible understanding of these basics of the Teaching leads to spontaneous and "non-volitional" living. That is the experiencing of the Teaching, the experiencing which is noumenal living. This experiencing soon leads to the immense awakening that this life is one great dream. Then we are enveloped in an overpowering sense of self-effacing unity. What could be left thereafter but the non-volitional witnessing of all that happens during the remainder of our allotted span?

Such non-volitional witnessing - witnessing all that happens without judging - arises along with a non-objective relation both to oneself and to others. A non-objective relation to oneself occurs when there is no thought of oneself as an object of any kind, physical or psychic. To know what one is without the slightest need of any explanation from anyone, to have the deepest possible conviction that oneself is totally devoid of any "trace-element of objectivity", is to experience the Teaching. The total lack of any objective quality can only mean the absence of the very concept of both the presence and the absence of the perceptible and the conceivable. A non-objective relation to oneself naturally results in a non-objective relation to others, which means ceasing to regard all phenomena, sentient or insentient, as objects of oneself. There is then an instant apperception that both the supposed subject (oneself) and the supposed objects (others) exist only as appearances. The result, in other words, is the elimination of the misunderstanding known as "ignorance", which means in effect the realization of our true nature.

Speaking as "I" (noumenon), we can all - each one of us - say to our phenomenal selves, "be still and know that I am God". It is only when the phenomenal self is absent that the noumenal "I" can be present.

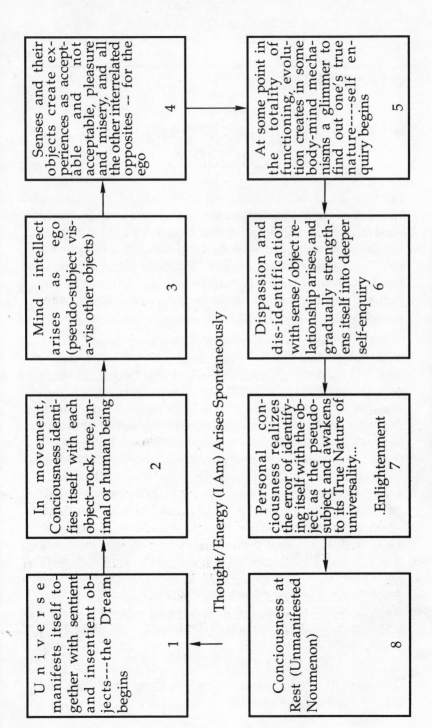

1

Universe manifests itself together with sentient and insentient objects--the Dream begins

2

In movement, Conciousness identifies itself with each object--rock, tree, animal or human being

3

Mind - intellect arises as ego (pseudo-subject vis-a-vis other objects)

4

Senses and their objects create experiences as acceptable and not acceptable, pleasure and misery, and all the other interrelated opposites -- for the ego

5

At some point in the totality of functioning, evolution creates in some body-mind mechanisms a glimmer to find out one's true nature---self enquiry begins

6

Dispassion and dis-identification with sense/object relationship arises, and gradually strengthens itself into deeper self-enquiry

7

Personal conciousness realizes the error of identifying itself with the object as the pseudo-subject and awakens to its True Nature of universality....

.Enlightenment

8

Conciousness at Rest (Unmanifested Noumenon)

Thought/Energy (I Am) Arises Spontaneously

CONCIOUSNESS AND MANIFESTATION

CHAPTER 1

• *SOME BASIC FACETS OF THE TEACHING*

I am quite aware that any kind of self-enquiry must start from the basic premise that I am not what I appear to be phenomenally. Perhaps the conditioning is too powerful, but apart from a clear intellectual understanding of the fact, I really find it extraordinarily difficult to *experience* the Teaching. I sometimes feel very despondent about it.

We shall go into the matter of the appearance of the reality presently. But first there is a simpler and more important aspect of the matter to be discussed. When this difficulty was brought up, Nisargadatta Maharaj used to ask a direct question: "Who is asking this question?" The split-mind presents the difficulty and seeks a solution in the same perverted context. It's a warped frame of reference. Maharaj would explain that you can perceive your body (at least a part of it) without the aid of a mirror and you can also watch thought presenting problems. It is a truism that the perceiver cannot be the perceived. Since the body-mind is a psychosomatic apparatus extended in space-time, the perceiver must be in another dimension which includes the volume that is in space-time. This dimension - which is the real you *(and every sentient being)* - must obviously be space-time itself, which includes the volume. In brief, the thought, the problem, is something totally apart from what-you-are. All that "you" can do is witness the arising of the problem, or more accurately, the problem can only be witnessed - like any scene on the road - without any involvement by "you".

I still don't understand why *you* think that *I* am not what I appear to be phenomenally.

The answer will present itself if you can tell me in your own ingenuous kind of way (in which people generally consider the subject) who you think you are.

With my simple mind, I say I am what is sitting here conversing with you.

You mean, an object - a tri-dimensional object - with a name which someone else has given it?

Anything wrong with that?

Nothing at all. There is no question of anything being right or wrong. But I would have thought that an object is only what appears as an image in someone's consciousness; that all objects, as images in the minds of "others", are mere inferences. What is more, science has come to the conclusion that the solidity of the body is itself illusory because the body is in fact nothing but a series of rhythmic wave functions, an emptiness, a throbbing energy.

I must confess that I feel quite stunned.

You are stunned to be told that what you have considered as a separate "self" is nothing more than an insignificant wave pattern. Undoubtedly it's an individualized wave pattern, but nevertheless, nothing more solid than a wave pattern with a name! That is because you have never considered yourself as anything other than the "solid" object with a name.

Even if science tells me I am only a wave pattern, it is not easy to disidentify myself from what I have always considered myself to be. Anyway, what am I then?

Doesn't it strike you that what you are is what everybody else is - Sentience? And therefore, instead of being a little "self" by way of an object, you are indeed everything!

You mean, instead of being a lowly clerk or even a millionaire (with his own worries), I own everything?

Well, that is so in a very general way, but not in a material sense. You don't *own* everything. You *are* everything.

This will need considerable deconditioning - and it will take some time.

No, it needn't. Apperceiving WHAT-IS, needs no time. Apperception *is* intemporality. It is the intellectual understanding in dialectics that needs time. If you were about to drink some liquid, and you were suddenly warned that it was poison, would you need time to apperceive the fact?

Could we pursue our talk about me being sentience rather than an object?

Yes, but I never said that the "me" which you have mentioned is not an object but sentience. What I said was that you, as "I AM", and every living thing that can feel "I" - *that* is sentience. Any kind of object is nothing whatever in itself; it is only something perceived. "I" alone am. "I" alone could BE - all else is perceived, and thus there cannot BE anything but "I".

What about subject/object?

Subject/object is just another object. It is nothing but the phenomenal object. "I" am beyond subject/object.

So you're saying "I" am pure noumenality, and not a thing of any kind.

"I" am not an identity that understands something "I" am that understanding itself.

****

Would it be possible to boil down the Teaching to its barest essentials?

Certainly. Would you like it in, say, four words - in fact, three?

Are you serious?

Of course I am. *"Non-existence of identity"*. That is the barest essential of the Teaching. There is really nothing else to be understood, since all other elements of the Teaching are dependent on that.

That seems simple enough.

Is it? Who is to bring about that non-existence of identity?

Obviously each of us, each individual.

What individual? Is it not understood that the individual is illusory, a mere appearance in consciousness?

Then who is to do whatever is to be done?

That is just the point. As long as there is a thing to be done, it is an utter impossibility, because non-existence of identity means the absence of anyone to do anything or to refrain from doing it.

You are taking me around in circles.

No, I am not. All I am doing - or appear to be doing - is trying to pull you out of the vicious circle. Once it is apperceived that there is neither any doing nor refraining from any doing, what remains is the *absence of all refraining* from any doing. That is the absolute absence of *any identity* (neither the existence nor the non-existence) to do or to refrain from doing anything whatsoever.

In other words, JUST BEing.

Right. Any attempted "doing" (positive or negative) turns the supposed do-er away from WHAT-HE-IS. Existence (or presence) means in truth, existence (presence) of existence (of presence), or existence (or presence) of non-existence (of absence). *Both existence and non-existence, or presence and absence, are concepts.* WHAT-IS or BEINGNESS is the absolute absence of both concepts, the absolute absence of both identity and non-identity.

I thought you said it was all very simple.

It is once it is apperceived. It is an astonishing fact that an extremely large majority of people - even those seriously interested in the subject - cannot get away from the idea that, whatever may be the essence of the Teaching, it is up to an identity to convince himself that in fact he is not an entity. At the other end is the extremely small minority that assumes that it is up to the non-entity to bring about the conviction that such is all that they are *as identities*! What this means is that all are firmly assuming that there is a non-identity! They seem to be in blissful ignorance that the non-entity becomes the entity they assume themselves to be!!! That is the whole problem. You must understand this. It is important.

Entity and non-entity are the inter-related opposite concepts. Is that what you mean?

Yes. Noumenality cannot include any concepts. What every seeker truly seeks - all do not realize it - is the absence of both the positive and the negative aspects of entity. But so long as there is any seeking - and thus the seeker - the absence of what is present as an entity (*positive or negative*) cannot happen. A self-anchored phenomenal object cannot possibly find the noumenon that it truly is, just as it is impossible for a shadow to find its substance. The apparent seeker in space-time is a concept. What is sought is another concept. So is the seeking and the finding (or non-finding). The absolute absence of all such concepts means the abandoning of the quest and such abandoning results in the annihilation of the seeker into BEINGNESS.

I believe Nisargadatta Maharaj once asked one of the regular visitors what she really wanted, and that he got very angry when she answered that she wanted nothing except enlightenment. Isn't that what everybody went to Maharaj for?

Yes, most of the visitors did go to Maharaj with the specific purpose and intention of getting liberated from the "bondage of *Samsara*". But, from the very start, and at all times, Maharaj dwelt on the fact that all is consciousness in which the totality of manifestation appears as phenomena. The human being is only a small part of that totality. He used to repeat continuously that the human being is only an appearance in consciousness like all phenomenal objects, that therefore, man cannot have any independent volition at all. And further, this assumed volition was itself the conceptual bondage. The regular visitor, if she had listened receptively, would never have given the answer that "she" did.

The very question whether so and so is ignorant or enlightened is totally misconceived because there is just no entity to whom (or to which) the conditions of ignorance or enlightenment could apply. What exists as an appearance is the psyche-soma. It's an appearance that is subject to the mechanism of phenomenality - i. e. duration - either on the basis of causality or on the basis of the more recent system of statistical probability. Such a phenomenal appearance cannot possibly be capable of exercising freedom of choice or action or anything else. And noumenality itself is wholly devoid of any objectivity.

What thinks it is in bondage (or free) is identified in thought with a phenomenal object, and *appears* to be in bondage or free. It is this thinking which is the real problem. *The "one" who thinks he is free is as much in bondage as the "one" who thinks he is bound.*

Then no concepts of bondage or freedom - or any concepts - would apply if there is only experiencing of the Teaching: stop thinking, stop conceptualizing, and JUST BE. Have I got it right?

You did have it right - until you framed the question in your mind and expressed it!

****

In spite of all that the Masters have said, in spite of having listened to you and Maharaj quite a few times, the question repeatedly pops up: Who is this "me" that constantly intrudes on all perceiving, all thinking, all feeling?

The vocable "I" - the "me" who thinks he is the volitional "do-er" - is what might be called the operational center in the phenomenal sentient object that is known as the human being. It's functional responsibility is to organize and care for the phenomenon it controls. This vocable "I", or the "me"-concept, attaches itself to the various emotional impulses that arise (like love-hate, fear, greed, etc.) for the protection and perpetuation of the phenomenon. It represents the psychosomatic mechanism, and this representation gives rise to the identification which is the cause of the supposed bondage. This operational center is called the "head" in Europe (what Wittington calls "the little man"), the "heart" in China (physiologically more relevant), and the "antahkarana" ("mind" including intellect, as the inner equipment) in India.

This operational center forms the "me"-concept, the self, the ego whose functioning is called "volition". It can only be a mere concept since the center, quite ignorant of its functional assignment, is as much a part of the psychic mechanism as the heart or the liver is part of the physical mechanism in the body. It assumes volition because it assumes responsibility for the emotions arising in the psyche. The vocable "I" (the ego) is thus merely inferential or conceptual and has no basis at all for any independent action as a thing-in-itself.

You mean, the assumption of responsibility (as volition) causes the identity, which in turn is the cause of the supposed bondage?

Quite so. Volition (and responsibility) is unnecessarily assumed for acts and events that are really subject to determination by what is called causation, the inexorable "law" of cause-effect. This assumption of responsibility is what causes the conceptual bondage, and the clear apprehension of the true position removes the identification and is called the conceptual liberation.

Is that all there is to the infamous bondage-and-liberation question?

The facts are there to be apperceived. The vocable "I" (the "me"-concept) cannot, by any kind of effort, ever be transformed into the subjective "I". The reason for the fruitlessness of the search for the subjective "I" as an object by an object should therefore be obvious. The subjective "I" is subjectivity itself without the slightest taint of objectivity. In brief, BEINGNESS (or IS-NESS) is necessarily the absence of both the interrelated phenomenal concepts of object and its subject. This BEINGNESS results through the superimposition and integration of both object and subject into nothingness, or the void of phenomenality (the plenum of noumenality).

****

Nisargadatta Maharaj sometimes said that the clear understanding of the nature of space and time is enough to understand the nature of the entire phenomenal manifestation. What precisely could he have had in mind?

Actually, Maharaj often said that a clear understanding of a single aspect of the manifestation and its functioning is sufficient for the purpose. What he had in mind was the fact that the unmanifest and the manifest (with all that the manifestation contains) is one concept and any distinction made is entirely inferential. It is like what happens when a dignitary is asked to unveil the portrait of another dignitary. The portrait is covered by one large piece of cloth and the arrangement is made so that by merely pulling gently at one end with a piece of string, the entire piece of cloth slowly moves away from the frame and reveals the painting. No part of manifestation could have been perceived unless it was extended in an apparent dimension called space, and it could not have been cognized unless it was extended in another dimension called time. In other words, no manifestation could have been perceived and cognized in the absence of space and time. This would seem to be an obvious fact, but the significance of it is that this space-time media, to which the sensorially perceptible universe is erroneously subjected, is not an objective reality, not a thing-in-itself. It is merely an inference, a concept, a psychic mechanism devised to make it possible to perceive the universe. And if the space-time, the necessary apparatus for the perceiving of the universe, is entirely conceptual, can the nature of the manifested universe be otherwise? Also, can the nature of the universe and the psychosomatic mechanism called the human being which forms part of it be anything but conceptual? This conclusion must lead us to the realization that space-time as well as the universe (and, of course, the human beings too) are truly that objective voidness which is non-manifestation, that potential plenum which is the unmanifest.

****

I have been intrigued by the fact that the unfortunate manifestations and other unpleasantries, both natural and apparently man-made, seem to be generally ignored in discussions about metaphysical matters. Why is that?

Constant change based on the interrelated concepts like love/hate, victory/defeat, birth/death, etc. are the warp and woof of the entire phenomenal manifestation. We see a love relationship suddenly change into hate and vice versa. Maharaj used to say that the love/hate relationship exists not only between sentient beings but also between planets, and that destructive manifestations like earthquakes, hurricanes and floods are the phenomenal effects of the "hate" relationship between the planets (the astrological predictions, though empirical, are based on planetary positions which reflect the love/hate relationship between them).

A cat eats a mouse, a lion devours a man, a man dines on a lamb, a cannibal feasts on a missionary, a soldier drops an atomic bomb annihilating an entire city. This functioning is interpreted as "good" by the perpetrators, while it is interpreted as "evil" by the victims. Each deed appears to each as his deed or his experience, but the fact of the matter is that no phenomenal object has any independent existence of his own. There is none to perform any deed, none to suffer any experience, and none to judge. There is only functionING which is manifested in this manner - and the noumenal subjective "I" *is* the functioning. The subjective "I", as the functioning, is devoid of attributes and therefore has no discriminatory faculty, while "responsibility" is a psychological concept based on volition that is non-existent.

Viewed from the individual's angle, problems will never cease; viewed from the angle of Totality, problems can never arise. Happiness and unhappiness are affective phenomena which appear to be experienced by things whereas the pure functioning of noumenality is totally devoid of discrimination. There is no do-er and no deed done. The subjective" I" is the DOING (the functioning) that is both the doer and what is done.

****

One of the most baffling - one might even say frustrating - things about the Teaching is the apparently contradictory statements Maharaj used to make almost in the same breath.

What did you expect? That the Teaching would be a sort of lazy mans guide to enlightenment? Consider the most compassionate Teaching of any Master to an earnest "seeker". It would contain so many enigmatical contradictions that the seeker would be quite baffled.

But Maharaj did say his Teaching was simple.

Did he say it was simple for anyone to understand? Did he not also say that it was simple for anyone who had a receptive mind and a higher level of intelligence? We must not forget that Maharaj, like other Masters, was trying to describe the indescribable, to express the inexpressible. Curiously enough the same kind of difficulty is found by the sub-atomic physicist in explaining his subject to a fresh student. Briefly, the difficulty boils down to the fact that words can function only in duality whereas their subject is non-duality.

Have you experienced any specific difficulty in regard to contradictions?

Well, consider for instance a statement like "noumenon and phenomenon are one", or, "form is nothing but void, void is nothing but form. "

It is because of such apparent contradictions, which are absolutely unavoidable, that phrases like "the gateless gate", "the pathless path", "effortless action", etc. , have come into active use. It is necessary to understand that it is not just a "grandstand" play on words.

Now consider the matter of transcendence and immanence as the classic contradiction, which it is so necessary to understand clearly. The mystery of transcendence and immanence existing together at one time lies in the fact that while noumenon is unicity, phenomena cannot take place except in duality so that there may be an observer and the object observed. On the other hand, there cannot be any phenomena without noumenon. The fact of the matter is that the noumenon and phenomenon, the unmanifest and the manifest cannot be different because manifestation is not the "creation" but merely the mirrorization of the unmanifest. The unmanifest Absolute must necessarily transcend the relative manifest because the Absolute is all there is. The relative is only its mirrorization. The Absolute must be immanent in the relative because the relative has no independent existence.

You mean the substance must necessarily and simultaneously transcend, and be immanent in, the shadow because the shadow cannot exist independently of the substance?

Right. Duality is purely notional inasmuch as phenomenality is the actual aspect of the pure potentiality of noumenality extended in space-time for its objectivization. Therefore, the Master has to say that since phenomena and non-phenomena are the same, there is neither phenomena nor non-phenomena.

"Then what is there?"

All there is, is Consciousness - in its potentiality when at rest, and in its actuality when in movement.

CHAPTER 2

- ## *THE DO-ER*

I was just thinking. . . .

That is too bad. Thinking is a pernicious habit.

I know you are always warning me against thinking or conceptualizing.

Quite. All that conceptualizing does is to make the "me"-concept stronger.

But how can we cease to think? Thinking is such a natural thing?

On the contrary. . . . As Ramana Maharshi and Nisargadatta Maharaj have both repeatedly stated, one in Tamil and the other in Marathi, "thinking is not man's nature". Thinking is an acquired habit. Granted, it's an old habit, cultivated from the first appearance of intellect in the child and reinforced regularly by the conditioning it receives at home, in school and elsewhere. Anyway, what is it that you were thinking about?

I was thinking that the trouble with us is that we keep in mind what-we-are-not and forget what-we-are.

This is what comes out of thinking - sheer nonsense.

Why, I thought is was rather sagacious.

There you go again! *Thinking* it was sagacious. Actually, thinking makes it otherwise.

Why?

"Sagacious" is necessarily untrue because it is relative. Whatever is relative is necessarily untrue. Have you not heard the wonderful statement of Lao-Tzu's that when you find something beautiful and good, the ugly and the bad are already there?

All I said was that the trouble with us is that we keep in mind what-we-are-not and forget what-we-are.

Would it be any better if you kept in mind what-you-are and forgot what-you-are-not? You would still be forgetting one and remembering the other - both relative terms.

Are you not making a simple thing complicated?

My dear fellow! This is a typical case of the thief shouting "stop thief"! WHAT-IS is truly simple. We make it complicated by our philosophizing about forgetting and remembering.

Anyway, what can I do?

Do nothing, as Nisargadatta Maharaj used to say. JUST BE. Anything a "me" *does* can not but be wrong.

Why?

Because a "me" is thought to be doing it.

You're really confusing me. You know that?

There's that "me again! I am sorry but it is certainly not my intention to cause confusion.

All right then. Just tell me, if there is nothing I should do, what should I *not* do?

Maharaj has already told us. JUST BE. Doing and not doing are both "doing" - one positive, the other the negative aspect of the "me's" volition. Trying to do something or not-to-do something brings in the illusory "me"-concept. It is always the "me" wanting to do something or not to do something with the idea of achieving. This is ridiculous because the "me" is the illusory ego without any entity. An illusion wanting to do or not to do something is absurd. The body is only an appearance in consciousness. How can an appearance achieve anything?

But if one is not to do or not-do anything, one might as well be dead.

How right you are - unwittingly of course! The "one" would be dead along with the split-mind of dualism. What would remain is the whole mind merely witnessing the functioning in totality of the phenomenal manifestation without any involvement. Therefore there would not be any of the inter-related opposites like happiness and unhappiness for the "me".

You mean when I rest content in JUST BEING, **the "me-concept" is absent.**

I do mean that. The "me"-concept means identification and therefore suffering. The absence of the "me" concept in pure witnessing means absence of involvement and therefore absence of suffering. The identified man takes part and suffers; the unidentified man merely watches the spectacle. The identified man tries to *understand* the Teaching; the unidentified man EXPERIENCES the Teaching.

CHAPTER 3

• *THINKING--A PERNICIOUS HABIT*

The other day, I casually mentioned that I was thinking and you said that was very bad.

Yes, I remember, I did say that thinking was bad.

Why?

Why? Because it is a pernicious habit which takes you away from WHAT-IS.

But how can you live without thinking? If I have to go somewhere, surely I must think how I should proceed, what way I should take, what plans I should make.

Of course you have to think when you are doing something. Even when you know that life is unreal, dreamlike, as almost every Master has been saying from times immemorial, life has to be lived *as if* it is real. So when thinking about something you are doing, you are not "conceptualizing", you are not creating images in your mind and therefore such thinking becomes a part of the "doing". When I said that thinking was a pernicious habit, I meant thinking which creates images in the mind. A mind creating images is always a split-mind thinking in dualism, thinking in terms of a subject/object, "me"/"not-me". Thinking is a pernicious habit because it creates separation as between "me" and the "other", therefore conflict, and therefore unhappiness.

Even assuming that thinking, other than the "doing-thinking", is done by the split-mind, that's the only mind I have, and that's what I have to use even to consider what I am told by the various Masters. Or do I have two minds - the whole mind and the split-mind?

Just ponder the words: you want to know if "I" have two minds, and which mind "I" should use "to consider" what has been said by the Masters! Who is the "I" who would "consider" what has been said by those who are one with WHAT-IS?

But surely the Masters themselves were, before they became one with the WHAT-IS, individuals like me who listened to what the Masters had to say.

Indeed they were. And that is precisely why they take the trouble to explain very simply that apart from the WHAT-IS, which Ramana Maharshi described as "I-I" (subjective "I"), all the "me"s and the "you"s are mere appearances in consciousness. They could not possibly be autonomous entities with independence of choice and decision. That would seem to be simple enough, precise enough and direct enough to preclude any "considering"?

Then what are we talking about? Why talk at all?

Why indeed?! That is precisely the reason that most Masters are not inclined to talk on this subject. That is precisely what Nisargadatta Maharaj meant when he said that he at once accepted his *Guru's* direct message "you are truly-*Parabrahman*" (noumenon), and that was it.

But Nisargadatta Maharaj did talk at regular sessions to visitors.

Of course he did. But he made it perfectly clear innumerable times, it was Consciousness talking to Consciousness; but more importantly, that so long as a visitor considered that he was an individual listening to Maharaj as another individual, he was wasting his time.

I am aware that Maharaj used to make this statement repeatedly, and I have wondered what he really meant.

It is quite simple really. When the listening is done by the individual, it is the mind-intellect that does the listening and it is of the nature of conceptualizing. When the listening is done by Consciousness, the individual is absent in such listening and then it is of the nature of EXPERIENCING. In other words, while intellectual listening is "*considering* the Teaching", listening without the individual present is "EXPERIENCING the Teaching".

Could you say something more about it?

Maharaj's point was very clear. Intellectual listening is done by the individual who in fact is merely an image in the mind. What this amounts to is perceiving *this* that is objectivized, and such perceiving prevents the apperceiving of *that* WHICH-IS. When the individual ("me"-concept) is absent in the listening with the whole mind, the separation between the listener and the listening is lost. The listening then becomes part of the totality of functioning without any interference from the split mind. Then, as Maharaj used to say, his words hit the target like an arrow because the path of the arrow was not blocked by the "me"-concept.

So the intellectual listening is done by the split-mind, while the listening which amounts to "experiencing the Teaching" is done by the whole mind?

That's exactly it.

It is clear that conceptualizing must stop. It is also clear that such thinking or conceptualizing is based on the "me" concept. But how can I stop this conceptualizing?

I shall repeat your question and I am sure you will find the answer in the question itself. "how can *I* stop conceptualizing?"

You mean the "I" who wants to know is itself the "me"-concept on which all conceptualizing is based?

Indeed I do. Any answer would necessarily be in the framework of conceptualizing. Also, the question implies an effort to be made by the same "I" who is in reality merely an image in someone's consciousness.

How is this dilemma solved?

The dilemma solves itself when it is analyzed and understood in its entirety. The *intuitive* understanding of the futility of any so-called effort by a so-called individual entity turns thought back from its usual outward flow to its source (the WITHIN, which itself is THAT-WHICH-IS). Such apperception, comporting as it does the spontaneous abandoning of the very attitude of wanting to make the imagined effort as a volitional act (which is in effect nothing other than conceptualizing), takes "one" to the very essence of "one's" being, the phenomenal absence of any "one" which is at once the noumenal presence. *Apperception, by its very nature, is impersonal.*

I'm still bothered by the basic difficulty that thought is the culprit, since without the thinking, without the mind, it is impossible to understand the problem in depth.
In any event, I accept that it's a fact that any positive effort to still the mind is bound to be an exercise in futility. What now?

Nisargadatta Maharaj had a supremely simple solution. Any effort to control the mind would only widen the split in the divided mind. But, he continued, *you are not the mind*. It is axiomatic that the perceiver can not be the perceived. You can perceive your body, therefore you are not the body. You can perceive your thoughts, therefore you are not the mind. You can witness the thoughts that come and go, and such witnessing will not be of the mind, if there is no involvement by way of volitional reactions like comparing and judging. Such witnessing will be of the same nature as the witnessing of the traffic on the road (that is until the mind "stops" in its natural flow because of some particular object attracting attention). It will simply "be there" like the chirping of the insects, or the cry of a bird. In such witnessing is apperception of what life and existence is all about. Volition is absent and life is accepted, with all that it brings. There is no separation between the acceptable and unacceptable.

CHAPTER 4

• *ENLIGHTENMENT - LIBERATION - REALIZATION*

I have read *Pointers*. I have also read *I Am That* [1]. I am rather intrigued by the assertion that you made in *Pointers*: "Awakening cannot take place so long as the idea persists that one is a seeker ". As I understand it - and probably the way most seekers understand it - it *is* the seeker who seeks enlightenment or awakening or liberation or *moksha* or by whatever name freedom from bondage is called. What exactly did you mean ?

Let me first explain what is understood by the term "seeker" so that there will not be any misunderstanding. The term "seeker" refers to an individual phenomenon who considers himself to be in bondage and seeks liberation or realization.

Yes, that is what I also understand by the term. Most of the scriptures specifically say that it is the individual who is caught in the net of *samsara* and must, by his own efforts and through the guidance of the *guru* and the study of the scriptures, liberate himself.

---

1   Sri Nisargadatta Maharaj, *I Am That* (Bombay: Chetana, 1973)

What we regard as scriptures today, were at one time written by some human being, in your terms some enlightened human being, and when he wrote that scripture, or gave his talks, he must obviously have had certain people in mind to whom his words were addressed. It would therefore not be right to accept such words as suitable for all types of people. Then as time passes, there is the inescapable danger of various interpolations being made, and certain inconvenient portions being deleted to suit the changing conditions and circumstances. Perhaps this is one of the reasons that Nisargadatta Maharaj preferred not to refer unduly to the scriptures. All he asked was that the listener keep an open and receptive mind. It would be a waste of time to listen to him with a mind that was burdened with a lot of accumulated concepts. Maharaj talked from his own experience.

I can understand what you say about the scriptures. But I find it difficult to accept the proposition that the seeker and what he considers as his efforts are both irrelevant to the attainment of awakening.

Perhaps we could follow Maharaj's method of beginning at the starting point and see where our meditation on the subject leads us.

The starting point would still be the seeker, would it not?

Indeed it would. But it would be necessary to throw the floodlight of enquiry on the seeker and find out exactly who or what he is. We would then examine if there is anything to be attained and if so, the means of attaining it.

That would be a wonderful experience. But, before we proceed, can I ask you a personal question? Are you enlightened?

The answer to your question is really contained in the enquiry we have undertaken, but to satisfy your curiosity at the very start, the answer is "yes". I do not want you to feel that your question has been sidetracked.

I am grateful for such a direct answer. Please go on.

Let us start with the proposition that all "you"s and all "me"s are merely appearances in consciousness. And further, that the totality of the manifestation (of which all sentient beings are an intrinsic part) and its functioning is like a dream.

Yes I can accept that - at least intellectually, and dialectically. It has been made clear both in *Pointers* and *I Am That*.

If that is accepted then the rest is easy. No individual who has been considered "enlightened" has ever himself had any pretensions that he was enlightened, although *others* might think he is enlightened. If any individual considers himself enlightened, then he is not.

Why so?

Because the pre-condition of enlightenment is that the identified individual self must be annihilated. No self or phenomenon has ever been enlightened.

Does that amount to saying that no one has ever been enlightened?

Yes it does. How could any "one", any "you" or any "me" possibly become enlightened? Of course, a phenomenon - a psychosomatic appearance in consciousness - could certainly *imagine* that he has become enlightened. Precisely as a dreamed phenomenon does in a dream, until he disappears along with all the other phenomena when the dreamer awakes.

But we do talk about sages being enlightened.

We certainly do, but that is part of a lot of nonsense we generally speak and get involved in! Thus it is said that the Buddha attained nirvana. But the Buddha himself said specifically that he had not *attained* anything. Ramana Maharshi repeatedly stated that what people usually call "realization" or "enlightenment" already exists. It is not something to be acquired. Therefore, any attempt to attain it would be a self-defeating exercise. But did his visitors believe him?

Apparently not. The search by seekers for attainment, and various intense discussions about the best methods for attaining, seem to continue unabated. Why is that?

The conditioning which is forced upon a child, at home and in schools ever since the dawn of intellect, is so powerful that even the word of a sage is not enough to remove it. Indeed, the pressing message of most of the Masters (including Nisargadatta Maharaj and Ramana Maharshi) - that liberation is nothing other than the removing of the illusion of bondage - seems to have had little effect.

Then what precisely is it that the seeker is seeking?

As Nisargadatta Maharaj used to say, what is sought is liberation or enlightenment or whatever, *as an object*. One by which they could, *as separate entities*, enjoy the pleasures of this world fully and totally without any dilution.

You mean we are really afraid of losing ourselves, our individual identifications?

Precisely so. The seeker sees no point in being enlightened if there is no one to enjoy that state of enlightenment!

If you put it that way, there seems to be some strength in that viewpoint.

"Seems" is correct. As I just said, the conditioning is so strong that what is simple and obvious appears complicated and obscure.

We would seem to be at an impasse. If enlightenment to most is a sort of symbol (a conceptual construct of what we are), then we cannot be what we are until and unless we give up the wrong notion of what we think we are!

That is very well put. Without the "me"-concept you will feel lost, and with it you will never find WHAT-YOU-ARE!

What is the solution?

The solution is in the realization that you already are what you are trying to become. It's in the seeing that there could never be a "me" to be enlightened.

In other words, "letting go" of the "me"-concept.

Exactly. *But*, this "letting go" cannot be achieved. It can only *happen* as a consequence of a deep conviction.

How can this deep conviction arise? Presumably, it cannot be achieved either.

Having arrived at this conclusion is itself the first step - if such it can be called. But each Master had his own intuitive "trick" to jerk the split-mind back into its wholeness. Thus, if the Zen Master found his disciple very seriously using his split- mind to argue himself into the corner of an *impasse* he would look out the window and make some irrelevant remark, like "how well the plants in the garden have grown". The effect would be to make the split-mind stop with a jolt.

Or, Nisargadatta Maharaj making a remark like "the seeker himself is what he is seeking".

Quite so. As I said, every master has his own trick which, let us understand, is used spontaneously and never contrived. One of these I like very much is that of the Chinese sage who, when asked "what is great *nirvana*?" is supposed to have answered, "great *nirvana* is not to commit oneself to the karma of birth and death;. " When further asked, "what is the *karma* of birth and death?", his answer was "to wish for great *nirvana* is the *karma* of birth and death"! This would apparently seem as utterly frustrating as Nisargadatta Maharaj saying that the seeker was wasting his time because there was nothing to be sought. How could the wish for *nirvana* itself be the bondage? The answer lies in the word "wish". It is the wish that is the cause of bondage, irrespective of whether the desire is for some material benefit or for liberation.

It is only apperception, an intuitive understanding of WHAT-IS, the apprehending of the non-duality between the manifest and the unmanifest, of the non-being of any individual as a separate entity to need any enlightenment, which brings about the realization of our true nature. Only this removes the misapprehension about bondage and liberation. Only then are both seen as mere concepts and therefore incapable of creating either bondage or liberation.

If there is no "me" to be enlightened, why all the excitement about the state of enlightenment?

All the excitement exists because the conditioning in man has inverted his viewpoint to an extent that makes him think that the abnormal condition of chaos, unrest and conflict is his normal state. He thinks that the normal state of unfathomable peace and contentment (glimpses of which he occasionally gets in those rare moments when the mind is free of thoughts) is an abnormal state that must be acquired or attained by special positive efforts.

You mean what is considered as the state of enlighten-ment is man's normal birthright which he has forgotten? That in order to regain that birthright, what is needed is not any positive doing to attain anything, but merely the abandoning of *this* conditioning which prevents the knowing of *that* original state?

That is it precisely. Nothing more and nothing less, which Nisargadatta Maharaj said in two words: JUST BE. Appercep-tion of this means, in effect, experiencing the Teaching.

That is all there is to it? And all the fuss that is made about enlightenment and realization. . .

Leads only to the obfuscation of what is essentially simple and obvious. As Ramana Maharshi said, "realiza-tion" or "liberation" is nothing other than "ridding yourself of the illusion that you are not free". The same thought was expressed by an ancient Chinese sage as "never having been bound, you have no need to seek deliverance. "

Let's see if I have this right. When the human being, that is really a phenomenal object, becomes aware of WHAT-IT-IS, he or it is then enlightened or awake or liber-ated, or whatever you want to call it?

Almost, but not quite. The situation could be described more accurately by saying: "Enlightenment occurs when what the phenomenal object is nonphenomenally, becomes aware of WHAT-IT-IS, via the phenomenal object". No phe-nomenon *as such* can ever become enlightened.

So really my earlier question "are you enlightened?" was misconceived!

Precisely like asking someone "have you stopped beat-ing your wife", when he not only had never beaten his wife, but he never even had a wife!

I just realized that there is an inherent misapprehension in the statement "enlightenment cannot be attained because we have always had it. "

How do you mean?

Well, it suggests that enlightenment is a thing or object.

True and the more basic point is that the absence of enlightenment as an object means the absence of its subject. Therefore, the misapprehension consists not only in the fact that enlightenment is not an object to be attained but that, more importantly, there is no "one" as a subject to attain enlightenment. Or anything else for that matter.

That brings us back to square one. What then are we?

The answer is provided by the Chinese sage Hui-Hai when he said that "enlightenment" was a means of being rid of conceptual thinking. Is that not a sufficiently clear answer to your query?

Do you mean that we *are* the conceptual thinking?

Of course "we" are the conceptual thinking which enlightenment suddenly gets rid of.

So that what remains is just enlightenment which can only be a noumenal "I".

Precisely - the noumenal "I" without the slightest touch of any objectivity or temporality.

In other words, there has never been - never can be - any "us" to do anything, to attain enlightenment or to be freed from any bondage. It is fantastic, utterly unbelievable.

Why is it unbelievable? Because "we" cannot have it? Because "we" cannot work hard at it? Because the conclusion is ineluctable that "we" ARE the enlightenment that "we" have been seeking? Because the seeker turns out to be what is sought? Ramana Maharshi has clearly stated that "there is neither creation nor destruction, neither destiny nor free will, neither path nor achievement". The same message has been repeated by many sages in different parts of the world at different times, including my *Guru* Nisargadatta Maharaj. But instead of BEING that Teaching, "we" want it as an object!

CHAPTER 5

• *DREAMING AND AWAKENING*

Life has often been cavalierly compared to a dream, and enlightenment to the awakening from the life-dream. Now, my difficulty is this: If the individual human being is merely a phenomenal object in someone's consciousness, how can this phenomenon dream, and how can it be awakened?

What a beautiful question! The sentient being as an object is only a phantom, a mere psychosomatic mechanism through which only illusory images can be produced. The interpretations of these images are generally known as persons and events in life. This means in effect that all actions and movements that are sensorially perceived - in fact, all phenomenal existence can only be figments of imagination (of mind, in consciousness).

In other words, although we may think of ourselves as autonomous entities, we are actually nothing more than dreamed characters. While the dreamed characters are seen as such when we (as the sleeper) wake up, we are still asleep in the living dream. But who wakes up from the living dream?

Nisargadatta Maharaj gave me the answer when I asked him this specific question, but not before chastising me with the remark, "you should know better than to ask a silly question like that". The answer, of course, was: "Who can it be but the consciousness, the personal consciousness as the dreamer, which has identified itself in split-mind with its own dreamed object, (the individual psychosomatic mechanism) as the pseudo-subject?".

It is therefore always the identified, individualized dreamer that awakes, never his dreamed object whether in the personal dream or the living dream. How can there be awakening for the dreamed object?

In other words, it can never be the sentient being who awakes?

Not quite correct. It is correct if by the "sentient being" you mean the being, the psychosomatic apparatus, but wrong if you understand that the sentient being is really sentience. An apparatus without sentience is dead matter. It is sentience or consciousness that has mistakenly identified itself with the apparatus (which is the dreamer) which awakes when there is realization of the mistaken identity.

So then awakening is in effect a sort of dis-covering (by removing the cover of *maya*) that what *appears* to be objective is in fact subjective.

Awakening is the disappearance of appearance, like the disappearing of the illusion of the substantiality of a mirage or a rainbow, with knowledge of the nature of the appearance which causes an optical illusion.

Does it mean then that in either dream the dreamed object is totally different from the dreamer?

No. Awakening means realizing that what is apparently objective is truly subjective. The dreamed-object cannot be anything other than its source; the dreamer, the consciousness, that is dreaming. The point is that the dreamed-objects cannot have any nature of their own other than that of their source. The shadow has no nature of its own other than that of the substance without which the shadow cannot occur.

So everything in the dream is the dreamer thereof. Thus the dreamed object (the illusory individual sentient being) is the sentience of consciousness (the dreamer).

Quite correct. But let us not forget that the dreamer, the consciousness, itself is not an object and so does not have any nature of its own, other than as a mere reflection of its own source, the Noumenon. It is for this reason that the Masters have always asserted that there never has been any creation or destruction. As Nisargadatta Maharaj constantly repeated, the whole universe and everything in it is an illusion, like "the child of a barren woman".

What does "awakening", in the final analysis, actually mean?

"Awakening" means that total disappearance of all phenomenal problems, resulting in a perpetual feeling of total freedom from all worries. It is a feeling of lightness, of floating in the air, untouched by the impurity - and confusion - of the split mind. It is as if the very root of all problems has been demolished, as if the Hydra has been fatally pierced in the heart to prevent the heads from growing again and again.

In other words, as you have said elsewhere, the problems will never cease from the viewpoint of the individual, but, from the viewpoint of Totality, problems can never arise.

Quite so. You might say that awakening is in effect the experiencing of the Teaching.

One last question. You said that asking someone if he is enlightened is like asking him if he has stopped beating his wife, though he had never beaten his wife. He was never other than enlightenment itself. Nevertheless, I would like to know what happens to the "phenomenal object" after there has been "awakening".

On awakening, the *identification* with the phenomenal object disappears. The phenomenal object itself continues to live phenomenally during its alloted span of duration, at the end of which it "dies" and is disposed of by burial or cremation. The consciousness that was in movement merges with the consciousness at rest. The awakened, after being awake for the rest of phenomenal life, finally falls into the deep sleep of the Noumenon - phenomenal presence becomes phenomenal absence and noumenal PRESENCE.

During the continuation of the life span, the dreamed character - the dreamer - exists only as an object in the living dream of "others" who are as yet unawakened. The awakened knows that "he" himself is the awakening. There is the apperception that he is the pure unconditioned subjectivity by means of which he and all sentient beings were dreamed. In fact, the dreamer, on awakening, finds that there never was a dreamer, only the phenomenon of dream-ING.

What this means then is that the living dream is merely an objectivization in consciousness, in which neither the dreamer nor the apparent dreamed entities could possibly have any independent existence.

Quite so. You started your questioning by saying that life has often been "cavalierly" compared to a dream. Actually, almost all Masters have compared the manifestation to a dream, not cavalierly but very seriously and quite literally. Indeed, the sage Vasishtha has categorically stated that there is no difference between the personal dream and the living dream. The dreaming takes place in consciousness. All objects, all appearances are dreamed. Perception and its conceptual interpretation takes place through the sensorialized phenomena who are also dreamed objects.

Are you saying that objects are essentially nothing more than organs of interpretation, through whose interpretive operation the universe appears?

apparent dreamer/dreamed = non dual dreaming of sentience

<u>Yes</u>. The living dream is dreamt by the sentient beings. Their personal dreams are microscopic reproductions of the living dream, which each sentient being dreams in his personal life.

Does it mean then that the sentient being is the dreamer of both his personal dream and the living dream?

Certainly not! There is no dreamer as such - That is the whole truth. Indeed, it is the essence of the apprehension of what we really ARE. It would lead to a lot of confusion to think we are only "dreamed" because we are both dreamed and dreaming. There is no such dreamer separate from the dreamed. There is only dreamING, the functioning of Consciousness. There is no entity to perform, nor is anything performed. There is only spontaneous actING, a sort of non-action because there is no actor.

Could you make it a little simpler?!

Perhaps it could be conceptually considered as this:
(a) There is only ONE DREAM without a dreamer.
(b) THAT-WHICH-WE-ARE is the dreamING.
(c) Each "me" is dreamed, and each "me" dreams a personal dream based on the personal "self".
Briefly, "I" am the dreaming of the universe, and "you" perceive it as a sensorialized phenomena, a dreamed object. "I" being the dreamer and the dreaming of the universe, would necessarily be awake in order that the dreaming may occur.
Perhaps you would prefer to have it put another way:
You wake up from you personal dream into the living dream. It is only in deep sleep that there is no dreaming at all because in deep sleep there is no "me". And the apperception of this fact means awakening from the living dream to WHAT-IS.

I am none of the phenomenal dreamer/dreamed; dreaming exists moment by moment within this one "I" am. Phenomenal presence implies noumenal Ground; "I" am this.

CHAPTER 6

• "REBIRTH" CONSIDERED

Nisargadatta Maharaj did not believe in rebirth in spite of the fact that most Hindu scriptures are agreed that there is rebirth. What is your feeling about this?

Maharaj always said that he spoke out of conviction and experience. He made it clear that what he said was not always based upon what the scriptures said. Maharaj's Teaching did not - indeed it could not - accept the concept of rebirth. A body can be said to be "born" and it can be said to "die", precisely as the words indicate. The body is "born", it grows into maturity and then on to old age, until it finally "dies" - that is to say, the body dies and decays underground, or is cremated and turns to ashes. The body, after death, is irretrievably and totally dissolved. The body therefore cannot be re-born. The breath, after death, mingles with the air and the sentience mingles with the universal consciousness.

Anything other than the objective can only be the subjective. And the subjective cannot "exist" as subjective because it is formless. The only form of existence is that which is objective - and the body cannot be reborn after it has been dissolved. The subjective, or more accurately, the non-objective obviously cannot either be born or die, let alone be reborn. So what is there to be reborn?

What about the "soul" or the psychic body or whatever it is that is supposed to be subject to *karma* and therefore to be reincarnated in another body to fulfill the effects of the *karma*?

You refer to the belief in an *animus* that may suffer birth but is never subject to death, and passes from one body to another in the apparent sequence of time. But surely such an animus must be an object (the non-objective is obviously not concerned in the antics of any object), and an object can only be a concept, and nothing else. In other words, the animus, as an object, is only a concept; and on the other hand, any entitification (and re-entitification on rebirth!) of subjectivity is ridiculous because subjectivity does not have even a touch of objectivity, and thus could have no "ens".

How did the notion of rebirth arise at all if the whole thing is so ridiculous?

It is identification with an imagined and spurious independent entity that is supposed to be born, to suffer and die. Identification incurs the process of causality called *karma* and also causes the notion of being in bondage to arise. It is always the entity that is spurious - the phenomenon, as its name implies, is merely an appearance in consciousness that can be neither bound nor free.

Did not Maharaj sometimes refer to "thousands of lives" in various contexts?

Yes, he did, but the reference was obviously to the process of evolution. Maharaj often referred to the dream play that life is. In this temporal dream play where sentient beings are created and destroyed in thousands every minute, evolution must obviously form the basis of the play of *Nisarga* (Life). In the physicist's bubble chambers, infinitesimally small high energy "elementary" particles (many of which have a lifetime much shorter than a millionth of a second) collide and annihilate each other or create new particles that give rise to a fresh chain of events in manifestation. Similarly, every baby born would be expected to play a particular role in the dream play so that the play may proceed on its inevitable course. The sentient being, which as a mere appearance in consciousness cannot possibly have independent choice of action, is created in order to fulfill a particular function (whether as a Hitler or a Gandhi or an insignificant individual) and not the other way around. It is not that a new function is created just so that the individual soul or animus (or whatever) be punished or rewarded for his *karma* in a previous birth! The supposed individual in any case is not an independent, autonomous entity, - he merely carries out his *destined* function which paves the way for the destined function of another supposed individual in the temporal future, according to the scenario of the dream play. There would necessarily be continuity between the form that dies and the new form that is born because evolution must go on, and nature does not start from scratch each time. This is no doubt the reason why Mozart could compose music when he was twelve and Jnaneshwar could produce the *Jnaneshwari* at the age of sixteen. But there is no reason for a conceptual individual to identify himself with a series of births in the temporal manifestation.

Did not the Buddha preach rebirth?

No, he did not. Indeed, the Buddha has said, "As there is no self, there is no transmigration of self; but there are deeds and continued effects of deeds. These deeds are being done but there is no doer. There is no entity that migrates, no self is transferred from one place to another; but there is a voice uttered here and the echo comes back. " Could it have been said any better or any clearer?

If the theory of rebirth and *karma* is to be accepted, the question inevitably arises: On what *karma* was the first human being based?

Quite so. All problems arise only when the basic fact of phenomenal manifestation is ignored: the entire manifestation is just a concept. Nothing is created, nothing is destroyed. The sages have said so from time immemorial. And, most Masters do not even refer to the matter of rebirth in their purest Teaching.

CHAPTER 7

• ## *THE INHERENT IDENTITY*

Is there one single aspect of the Nisargadatta Teaching which would cover the entire Teaching? Is there something, a clear understanding of which would bring about the experiencing of the entire Teaching?

I can tell you what Maharaj himself considered the very core of his Teaching. Indeed, Saint Jnaneshwar in his *Amritanubhava* gave a very apt simile: a loosely tied *dhoti* - when one end of it is given a pull, all the rest of it comes loose. This master key is the clear apprehension of the inherent identity of conceptual opposites. Maharaj said that the apprehension of even one pair of such interdependent counterparts is itself liberation, adding that to "see" one is to "see" all. His assurance is based on the fact that this perfect apprehension will result in immediate disidentification with the "me". The "me" being the pseudo (phenomenal) subject of pseudo (phenomenal) objects, both of which are mere concepts without any nature of their own. The mutual annihilation of both these concepts unveils the noumenal functioning which is all there is.

How does this disidentification come about?

It does not really matter whether the concepts refer to object and subject, phenomenon and noumenon, or presence and absence or any other pair of opposites. All are concerned with the splitting of the mind (called dualism) in the process of conceptualization and this is the supposed bondage. The absence of this process of dualism, non-dualism (a-dvaita), which implies mind upstream of all conceptualizing, is supposed freedom or liberation as it denotes a return to the original wholeness of mind. It implies disidentification with a phenomenal object, the earlier identification with which had involved the splitting of the whole-mind into the dualism of a pseudo-subject and pseudo-object. Thus the split-mind dualism is the supposed bondage, the return to wholeness is liberation. It is the assimilation of the interrelated opposites - a superimposition - that results in their mutual cancellation or negation. But it can never result in their union, because it is psychologically impossible to unite two contradictory thoughts. It is the *negation* of the interrelated self-contradictory opposites which results in a wholeness that is conceived as a void. It is important to realize - and Maharaj gave great importance to this point - that the void resulting from assimilation is a void that continues to be a concept, which itself has to be negated in order to realize our true nature. In other words, the essential negation is the further negation of the result of the negation of presence and absence.

I can intuitively feel the truth of what you are saying, but could you put it a different way so that I might understand it intellectually?

That sounds queer - usually the difficulty expressed is that something is intellectually understood but found difficult to accept! Let me put it this way. . . but please remember the basic inadequacy of any explanation:

The void that results from the assimilation or superimposition of the two opposites of presence and absence has to be known to "something"; otherwise there would be no absolute PRESENCE. The mutual negation of knowledge and its interrelated opposite has to be known to some KNOWLEDGE that has existed upstream of the conceptual pair of opposites, knowledge and ignorance. KNOWLEDGE is the substratum of all conceptualization (and manifestation). That sub-stratum, that substance, is the further negation (*neti, neti*) of the void resulting from the superimposition of knowledge and ignorance, of presence and absence. Consciousness is present during the waking state, absent during the deep sleep state or under sedation. But both these states of consciousness - (presence and absence) - are known to the ever present AWARENESS. To put this in another way, if some photographic image is projected on to a screen and then switched off, the presence and the absence of the image, when assimilated, would leave a void. But the screen, the substratum on which the images appeared and disappeared, would still be there. It is this screen (of AWARENESS) on which occurs the presence and absence of consciousness. Our real nature is the AWARENESS which is the absence of the absence (of void) resulting from the cancellation of both presence and absence.

What is the significance of Maharaj's statement that clear apprehension of the inherent identity of even one pair of opposites is itself enlightenment?

The significant point about the negation of the opposites is that all the pairs of opposites can be grouped and analyzed under the single aspect of negative-positive. The subsequent annihilation of the resultant void-concept can come about only when the conceptual dualities are considered in their personal aspect of "you" and "I" (me). This is because the resultant voidness is a personal one which can only be further abolished by the negation of both the pseudo-subject and its object. Such negation of the personal voidness can be apprehended only by the immediate apperceiving that is noumenality, apperceiving at the unsplit source of phenomenality - without reification, without rationalization, without the interference of mentation. Saint Jnaneshwar in his *Amritanubhava* says that he could get such apperception only by the grace of his *Guru* (by the surrendering of his personal identity to his *Guru*).

What do you mean when you say that the dualities should be considered in the personal aspect?

Under the personal pronoun "I" (me) would come the group of negative elements (self, subject,*nirvana*, negative, non-manifestation, etc.) and under the personal pronoun "you" would come the group of positive elements (other, object, *samsara*, positive, manifestation, etc.).

The practical application of the difference between dualism and non-dualism, and the total abolition of this difference can be seen in the different perspectives of perceiving

(a) *phenomenal cognizing* where the pseudo-subject (the ignorant man) perceives pseudo-object;

(b) *noumenal cognizing* where phenomenality is cognized subjectively, i. e. object is seen as subject only;

(c) *non-dual cognizing* where phenomenality (object) and noumenality (subject) are seen as not separate - which implies the total demolition of all interdependent counterparts.

These are three stages in the conceptual evolution of enlightenment - ignorance, apperception and enlightenment. The sage comes to the final truth: the final negation of the conceptual void created by the negation of the "me" and the "not me" This is the "I-I" (subjective I) which is *both* the unmanifest and the manifest, *both* the transcendence and immanence.

You mean there cannot be "phenomena" without "noumenon" nor "noumenon" without "phenomena"?

That's it. "Phenomena" and "noumenon" might be said to be two aspects of non-conceptuality. Noumenon, as the source of everything, cannot be anything; and a phenomenon, being devoid of self-nature is no thing in itself but, as the emanation from noumenon, is everything. A deep understanding that neither can be anything but that everything is both - that forever separate as concepts, they are, when unconceived, eternally inseparable - is the experiencing of the Teaching. Indeed, that IDENTITY is itself this experience.

What precisely do you mean to convey when you say that the IDENTITY is itself the experiencing of the Teaching?

I should think that was self-evident. "Being" and "non-being" cannot *be* without the other. Therefore they can objectively exist only as two conceptual aspects of one whole which itself cannot be conceived as such because it is precisely that which seeks to conceive - that which we ARE. Where there is neither being nor non-being, neither appearance nor void, neither subject nor object, there has, therefore, to be IDENTITY, *which cannot perceive itself*. That is non-conceptuality. That is subjectivity. That is absolute awareness not aware of itself. That is what we ARE. WHAT-WE-ARE cannot be the object of what-we-are.

But we do conceive the pairs of opposites because "we" are then the divided mind, split into a subject/object relationship when the universal consciousness (which we are) identifies itself with the psychosomatic mechanism. But the split-mind (which is the content of consciousness) gets united into its wholeness when the identity of opposites is apperceived and the personal consciousness regains its universality.

Am I to understand then that phenomena are merely a projection by noumenon that could be ignored as illusory?

Phenomena are *not* something projected by noumenon because then they would be two separate things, each existing independently. Phenomena *are* noumenon in its objective expression; they are noumenon extended in space-time as its appearance. If you consider the phenomenal universe by itself and then decide that it is illusory, you will be making the basic mistake of not apperceiving the essential identity between the polaric opposites.

Where do we, as sentient beings, fit into these opposites?

In *this* appearance, which is an extension in space-time called manifestation, we are a part of the manifestation in which we, as sentient beings, have no nature of our own. But *that* functioning is itself what we sentient beings ARE, in which noumenality and phenomenality are identical. In what we ARE there cannot be any entity (which is a phenomenal concept) and no phenomenal object can have any nature of its own because it just does not exist. In what we ARE there is no duality, only an independent functionING, the manifesting of non-manifestation. In brief, *we are noumenality, extended in space-time, functioning as phenomenality.* Noumenality is necessarily incognizable because it is absolutely all that we are, whether non-manifested or in apparent manifestation. Apperceiving this is experiencing the Teaching.

CHAPTER 8

• *THE WHOLE TROUBLE*

Why does the Absolute not know itself? Many talks seemed to end with this question - and Nisargadatta Maharaj invariably replied with the question, "Where is the need for the Absolute to know itself?" He seemed to feel that the counter-question was all the answer that was necessary. What did Maharaj mean - and did he deliberately stop all further probing with that counter-question?

That is a lot of questioning! As was typical of Maharaj, deliberately or otherwise, he gave an answer so accurate that it really needed no further elucidation. Indeed, any further supplementary explanation could have clouded both the question and the answer! In this particular case, consider the question: Why does the Absolute not know itself? - the answer is that it *does not need to know itself*.

I'm afraid I still don't get it.

The question is not really understood in its implication, which is that "knowing" anything brings in an object to know. For the Absolute to know itself, the Absolute will have to objectify and that means that the Absolute is some *thing* that *does* some *thing*.

Also, when the Absolute thereafter ceases objectifying, there would then be no object and the Absolute could no longer be the subject. In other words, briefly, for the Absolute to know itself, a subject/object relation would have to be created. And this is absurd. Where is the need to establish such a relationship? Indeed, this is the whole trouble, the cause of all the trouble in the phenomenal universe - the subject/object relationship.

How do you mean the whole trouble?

Is it not the whole trouble? How could the Absolute be either subject or object? And for what reason? The Absolute is just Absolute - "I" is always just "I". The billions of "me"s are mere concepts, never objects because if the "me" were an object it would need *a* subject, whereas "I" am pure subjectivity. Such *a* subject would itself be an object and then "I" would no longer be "I-I". Do you see this point?

No!

Well, do you not see that the whole trouble from time immemorial has been that the "me", an illusion, has been searching for the Absolute which is I-AM. "I" am all that there IS or can be. How can there by any "me" or "you" or "him" or "her" in search of anything? All there is IS "I" - the seeker IS the sought.

Oh. Is this the "trouble" that Maharaj had in mind when he exhorted his listeners "not to scratch at a place and thereby produce an itch that was not there before?"

Right. And this is also the reason Maharaj's *mahavakya* was JUST BE.

And this is also what is meant by experiencing the Teaching?

Right. In brief, all questions including those such as "is XYZ ignorant or enlightened?" and "is XYZ's life predestined or does he have free-will?" are all based on a false premise - that XYZ is an autonomous entity with volition. The premise is incorrect, and so are all the questions based on that premise. If this is clearly apperceived, the apperception itself amounts to JUST BEING.

CHAPTER 9

• *WHO - WHERE - WHEN?*

I have always wondered why it is so difficult to accept the basic teachings of almost all the Masters of Advaita philosophy that the individual entity as such is wholly illusory.

Who is this "I" who has always pondered and wondered upon the problem?

I had a feeling you might ask that!

I am sorry, but it does seem to be a good point for an investigation or an exploration. When I first found Nisargadatta Maharaj doing it, I used to feel so terribly frustrated, but very soon I could see clearly that he was neither shirking the question nor trying to sidetrack me and confuse the issue. What he was doing was putting the matter into perspective at the very start, so that the dialogue would remain on an impersonal level and not turn into an intellectual debate.

In other words, the individual entity is pushed back into the background where it belongs, being only an illusion.

Quite so. That is also the reason why Maharaj repeatedly warned his listeners not to listen to him as one individual to another.

What exactly did he mean?

What he meant is that words, because of their inherent limitation, can hardly ever point at the Absolute when they are heard and interpreted in the context of phenomenal duality. The confusion becomes confounded when the words are not apprehended on the very firm basis that the listener is not what he thinks he is but an utterly unsubstantial illusory dream figure.

But is it really possible to do so?

Is it not possible, if you are interested in music, to listen to a performance without the intrusion of the individual listener - when the music and the listening are without any separation? But our conditioning is so powerful that even when the subject of our consideration is the non-existence of a self, our thoughts tend to get expressed in a manner that the sentient being as a medium is envisaged as having objective existence. It is for this reason that Nisargadatta Maharaj so often startled the questioner with a counter question: "Who wants to know?" or, "Who is asking this question?" Indeed, the very frustration this counter-question produced in the questioner was the proof that the dialogue was being based from the viewpoint of the individual as an objective entity!

I can see this very clearly. Our conditioning is such that whenever anything happens our immediate reaction is the query "who" or "whom" in regard to the occurrence. We do not accept an event on its own as just an event.

That is correct. As soon as one sees a book or a book is discussed, the query rises, "who has written the book?" If one sees a painting, instead of perceiving it on its own merit, we want to know who did it? What is more, our judgement on it would, consciously or unconsciously, be based on the reputation and standing of the painter.

But surely the painter is not irrelevant to the painting.

Is that really so? We are so used to thinking that nothing can happen without a "who" that does it, or a "whom" it affects, that we are inclined to forget that *all* events are movements in consciousness within the totality of functioning which is the active aspect (in time) of the totality of the manifestation (in space). We forget that all human beings are merely psychosomatic mechanisms through which the manifestation and its functioning is perceived and cognized.

All Masters have repeatedly asseverated in many different ways, in many different contexts, that there really is no such thing as a separate individual.

That there cannot be a separate individual is the very basis of all non-dualistic teaching and this is surely known by every seeker of the truth. Where does the difficulty lie?

Intellectually and dialectically a fairly high degree of comprehension of this basic fact is certainly not uncommon, but the fact of the matter is that such comprehension rarely reaches the degree of apprehension or apperception which denotes *experiencing* of the Teaching. This is because those who are satisfied with the relative intellectual understanding are not prepared - one might say, are afraid - to accept the total annihilation of their precious selves. They can accept that the *other* selves are illusory but they cannot accept that their own identity is also wholly illusory. Their sincerity would rarely be in question. Indeed, they would often be found working very hard at the various methods and techniques they have acquired from various sources (and they are continually searching for more). They don't realize that all methods and techniques are utterly useless unless they give up the illusion that they themselves are autonomous entities, with volition and choice, working towards a goal.

**What really happens after apperception that all phe-
nomena are appearance only? In other words, after the
"who", the identification with "me" as an object, is
demolished?**

After apperception, obviously the phenomenal "who" as
an *appearance* does not disappear (until death), nor does the
phenomenal universe disappear. But what does happen is
that the liberation, as a consequence of the dis-identification,
is not only from "who" but also from "where" and "when",
because for the phenomenal "subject", having known at last
what he has always been, and what the phenomenal manifestation has always been, these terms are all meaningless. He,
however, continues to use them as "others" do - the "others"
being as meaningless - just as he uses the term "the sun rises
(or sets)" which is meaningless but useful for communica-
tion with others.

So in fact there never has been a "who".

No, from the beginning there never could have been a
single "who". The "who", totally absent noumenally, has always been the ubiquitous "who" phenomenally. The "who",
the asker of the question, is both the seeker and the sought.

CHAPTER 10

• _WHAT HE THINKS OF ME_

Hello, you are beaming like a lamp. What's up?

Well, have you seen the latest copy of the Times? No? Don't bother. I have a copy right here. Page 5.

Ah, here we are. A photograph of you, a nice write up too. Is this chap a friend of yours?

He is now! Why are you smiling like that?

Was I? Like what?

Like you have something up your sleeve. Like the cat who ate the canary.

Oh, well. I was just thinking about "that bastard" who wrote a nasty piece about your book in some "rag" a few days ago.

Are you making fun of me? Wouldn't you be upset if someone said something rotten about you?

Of course not. Why should I be upset about a brickbat thrown at an image in someone else's (aspect of) mind. It's entirely his own creation and quite unrelated to the phenomenon ("me") to which the image is attached. In your own case, a few days ago someone threw a brickbat at an image of you in his mind. Today, someone else threw a bouquet at an image in his mind. The phenomenon, that is "you", has remained the same while the images in mind have been different.

How do you mean "images in mind"?

Dualistic discrimination in the process of functioning as "self" and "other". It's a universally condemned process, also known variously (in non-dualistic teaching like Advaita and Tao) as discrimination, false thought, objective seeing, etc.. It is the very mechanism of "bondage".

In other words, objectifying a purely subjective concept - creating an effigy and then throwing bouquets or brickbats at it.

That is well said. It should be remembered, however, that the understanding itself would preclude all "saying" - there is no need at all to express what is understood. It can only make the truth untrue.

I can buy that. But the theory aside, which is the real you - the one that deserves the bouquet or the brickbat?

You have missed the point. I could be not just one or the other, but a host of others as others might see "me".

You really are serious aren't you? This is not just theory for you, but actual fact .

Look. As "I", I am precisely nothing - no *thing*. I appear as whatever I am perceived to be. And this is as much "fact" as anything in phenomenal manifestation could be said to be. How could "I" be anything but I AM?

Let's be practical. Am I to understand that you have no personal identity, no personality at all? How can you live without one?Surely, you yourself must know what you are, even if someone else may not.

I'm not trying to be funny or clever. See for yourself. Why should my perceptual and conceptual interpretation of my appearance (which is "me") be any more valid or invalid, phenomenally, than that of any one else's. My own could well be perhaps a little more flattering and exaggerated, but certainly equally imaginary!

I would still like an answer. I am not just superficially curious. I am seriously curious.

I have so many "selves" and while some of them may be "good" - gentle, kind and noble many others would be "bad" - wild, cruel and obnoxious. Again, let me assure you, I am not being flippant. Actually the range of our "selves" in this waking-dream is very much more inhibited than in our sleeping dreams. In our dreams we accept ourselves for whatever we appear to be, and it is only in retrospect that we judge ourselves according to the "waking" standards.

You mean it is in this spirit of relativism that we should view what other people think of us?

Would not anything else be absurd? Whatever people think of me is *their* thought, visualized in their own aspect of the split-mind known as "memory". It is their mnemonic impression, which has nothing to do with me, with what I am or what I am not.

I find you amazing.

All that your amazement shows is that *my* appearance in *your* mind is not very flattering if you believed that I would care about what happens in a split-mind!

Phenomenally, then, are we nothing other than what is perceived?

Perceived - and conceived: a concept. Our supposed "self" is what "others" conceive; and of course "others" must include our own self-conceiving because each of us is an "other" supposed by a supposed "self". The point is that both the "self" and the "other" do not exist apart from being merely the mechanism of manifestation in duality as subject/object.

Then what are we?

Is it not obvious? We are, very simply, "I", eternally unaware of what I-ness is.

**What you say seems so clear and so obvious that it's dif-
ficult to see how it could be otherwise. As appearances we
can only be concepts in the split-mind, whether "ours" or
those of apparent "others".**

How could it be otherwise? Sages, men of vision, have
been saying so for thousands of years.

And yet people have not believed that!

The sages did not ask people to believe anything. Belief
is also a concept. They merely pointed to the truth.

But how are "selves" supposed to act?

"Supposed to act"? How can an appearance be supposed
to act?This was also told to us by the sages thousands of
years ago, though of course in words and terms prevalent
in their times. Therefore perhaps the need for books like this
one. Anyway, the "selves" do not "act" - they *appear* to *react*
to stimuli from outside, as images in mind.

**What precisely is the manner in which such apparent
reaction takes place?**

What they *appear* to do is conceptual interpretation of
such reacting, an apparent functioning that we call our
"living".

**But surely, if the "selves" are merely appearances in
consciousness, images in the split-mind, there must be
something behind them. What is that?**

This is the real trouble. I mean, trying to put into words
something that is indescribable turns it into a concept. Anyway, we may try to apperceive it by thinking of it as a

functioning which is spontaneous acting without any re-acting. That is the Taoist way of looking at it, and as good as any, and better than most.

How would you explain it?

I might perhaps say that THAT is transcendent noumenal-ity which is immanent as phenomenality (otherwise phe-nomenality would have no "substance"), objectifying what it is as what we appear to be through a process of dualistic manifestation in the conceptual extension of the media known as "space" and "time".

Where do we come in, in this functioning?

"We" as WHAT-WE-ARE, being all that *is*, can never be out of any functioning. As an appearance in the mind, we are nothing; As WHAT-WE-ARE, we are everything. Noumenon and phenomenon are not two, nor are they different. As I said, what they are is transcendence phenomenally and im-manence noumenally.

CHAPTER 11

• *WHO IS THE PERCEIVER WHO PERCEIVES?*

Is there a single factor that can be isolated as the one that prevents the apperceiving of our true nature?

Yes there is. In fact, Nisargadatta Maharaj gave the answer at one of his talks. The single factor that comes in the way of apperception is the incorrigible habit of viewing everything - every event - from the point of view of a "who" as the pseudo-subject and the "what" as the object, with a succession of "whom", "when", "where" , and "why". But then, this habit unfortunately gets strengthened by the fact that the message of the Masters is generally conveyed through nouns while the deepest meaning can only be suggested by verbs and adverbial forms. In other words, the Teaching is really concerned far more with functioning and its process than with the "who" that functions or with the "what" that results from functioning. Both the "who" and the "what" are incidental, inferential and almost irrelevant. Thus for instance, "living" in the world is a dream and the human beings are dreamed characters who, for all purposes, are only incidental as they have no independence or volition.

You mean while the message of the Masters is that what is objectivized, being an appearance, is not true, the language used is itself objective?

Right. It is necessary to keep this in mind when the Teaching is being conveyed in whatever form. At least to that extent the understanding will be more accurate. It is an interesting point, in the context of the use of parts-of-speech being a significant hindrance to understanding, that the Teaching of Indian *Mahayana* (which moved out of India a long time ago) is best studied in the written language of China in which parts-of-speech practically do not exist. There is no gainsaying the fact that Reality or Truth cannot be expressed at all, except to the extent that it can be suggested or pointed at. But to the extent that language must be used, care has to be exercised by both the speaker and the listener to remember that nouns point in the opposite direction and thereby create considerable misunderstanding.

Take the terms "time" and "space". They at once suggest "objects" whereas they are relative to the functioning which uses them as mere concepts. Also, the senses have relevance only to the extent that they are conceptualized to serve the functioning. The use of nouns for the senses - to an extent the use of nouns is, of course, inevitable - throws the essential functioning in the background, and brings the "who" to the front although "he" has no nature of "his" own. Thus, when "perceiving" is considered, the function of perceiving is ignored and importance is given to the "perceiver" and the perceived object.

What is the answer to the situation?

The answer is to remember constantly the circumstances which have brought about the situation. Focus attention on the essential functioning and relegate the dreamed characters, the puppets, the sentient beings to the background. It is for this reason, to show the utter illusoriness of the "who", that Nisargadatta Maharaj often used to interrupt the questioner and ask him "who wants to know". Maharaj would thus bring the questioner's mind back from the me-entity, "who", to the essential functioning which should receive the total attention. In deep sleep, there is no manifestation, no universe, no functioning, no "who" through whom the functioning takes place. All these arise into existence only when consciousness arises in the form of the waking state. Let us see what happens during the process of waking up in sort of "slow motion". In the early moments after waking up, consciousness retains its impersonal nature, particularly if the waking process is natural and you are not awakened into a sense of urgency by the alarm clock or by a person. This is particularly noticeable if you are out in the country and the process of waking up is allowed its normal full time. When the consciousness during this brief period retains its impersonal nature, the perceiving of the outer world is not tainted by dualism of subject/object, by the sense of "me"/"not me". But very soon the pseudo-subject "me" takes over and all perceiving is done by the "me". Even so, if we analyzed what is perceived, we would find that we can perceive "our" own hands and feet as being within the volume that is perceived, together with other parts of "our" bodies that would constitute objects to what is perceiving. But we cannot perceive that "which is perceiving". This is because what is doing the actual perceiving - "the perceiver" does not lie within that volume or space.

Are you saying that the perceiver - what is perceiving - is something outside the volume within which our psychosomatic apparatus, our body, can be perceived?

That would be the inescapable conclusion, wouldn't it? Since the perceiving subject perceives the volume of the perceived object, what is perceiving must necessarily be outside the objective dimensions constituting "volume". The question then is: who or what is doing the perceiving and where is it? As we have seen, this that is perceiving must be "beyond" the three objective dimensions of volume. In other words, just as volume includes area, so the center of perceiving must include volume. Also, this center must be *everywhere* and it also must be able to perceive all the time because the perceiving is done by some sentient being somewhere *all the time*. Therefore, this subjective perceiving center can be nothing other than infinity and intemporality - operating *here* and *now*.

But what about the perceiver to which each human being refers whenever he says "I perceive"?

With the analysis done so far, surely it should be possible to locate this personal perceiving center of each human being. If the subjective functional center - the infinity and intemporality - is the "I-I", surely the objective operational center must be the tri-dimensional psychosomatic mechanism with which each human being is identified as "me". In other words, *that* subjective extra-dimensional center, nameless and formless, is what we ARE as "I", while *this* objective tri-dimensional center - the *nama-rupa* (name and form) - is what we *appear* to be as "me" in space-time.

You mean what is phenomenally present is the psychosomatic apparatus representing "me" as the objective operating center, while what is phenomenally absent - because it is formless - is the subjective functional center that is eternal PRESENCE as the infinite and intemporal "I-I".

That is neatly expressed. Now all that is needed is the instantaneous apperception of it, without the need to express it.

CHAPTER 12

• *TRUE PERCEIVING*

One comes across the words "true perceiving" quite often. What precisely are they intended to convey?

True perceiving means perceiving phenomenality as such - and therefore the phenomenal objects - after apperceiving the identity of phenomenality and noumenality. Phenomenality is merely the extension of noumenality in space and time - they are not two. Noumenon has objectified itself into phenomenality so that it may be perceivable in space-time duality. True perceiving is therefore the perceiving of the true identity of subject and object. True perceiving is perceiving that there is factually no perceiver/perceived relation, only the function of perceive-ING.

True perceiving then would mean perceiving from the viewpoint of the subjective functional center and not from the viewpoint of the objective operational center.

Right. While the objective operational center is represented by the tri-dimensional psychosomatic appearance, the subjective center is formless, phenomenally absent, because phenomenal appearance in space-time would make it an object. The subjective center is present everywhere, all the time, and no "where", at no "time", because it is beyond space and time. It is infinity and intemporality - present HERE and NOW throughout eternity. In brief, true perceiving is perceiving that any perceiving between one sentient being and another can only be false perceiving because both are objects.

False perceiving?

The perceiving usually done by human beings is necessarily false because both the supposed subject and the perceived object are *objects*, appearances in consciousness. The
pseudo-subject himself becomes an object when he is perceived by another object posing as the pseudo-subject. And
when consciousness is absent, as in deep sleep or under
sedation, there cannot be any perceiving in this sense even
though the pseudo-subject exists. In fact all perceiving, as
imagined by human beings is false perceiving. True perceiving is really non-perceiving, the perceiving that is beyond
the body and thought. When there is true perceiving (consciousness perceiving the manifestation within itself), what
can there be to perceive? The entire manifestation is only the
objective expression of the one subject. Perceiving this is true
perceiving - the transcendence of the subject/object dualism.

Nisargadatta Maharaj was once asked if what he saw in
the world was different from what other people saw. His answer was that he saw the same things but the way of seeing
was totally different. He did not see the "other people" as
other people!

That is as accurate an answer as could be expected from
Maharaj.

**But what did the answer really mean? He did not ex-
plain further.**

Would he not have explained further if he thought it necessary?He must have considered that the explanation
should really present itself if meditated upon.

**Perhaps we could meditate upon it now in the form of
the talk that is now going on.**

Maharaj may not have given a detailed explanation, but
he did give a hint then, when he suggested that the questioner should look into the two mirrors in the room. Now
suppose there are two, three or more mirrors at different an-

gles before you. There would be several images in the mirrors but only one you. All movements of the images would be controlled by you, the images themselves would have no volition. Now also suppose you could bestow sentience in the mirror images so that they could "perceive" one another. Is it not clear that the perceiving of one another by the images, each as a pseudo-subject with the others as objects, would be false perceiving? True perceiving is only that perceiving done by the subjective center outside the mirrors, the true subject. In fact, this true perceiving is really *no-perceiving* because all there is, is the ONE subject without any objects. If the subject could see another object that has independent existence, the subject himself would be the object!

True perceiving is, therefore, the turning back of the split-mind from outward objectifying (which is what perceiving in dualism means), inward, to its wholeness or back to non-objectivity from which arises the objectivity.

The simile of the mirror gives rise to various difficulties. . .

Of course it does. And that is why the Masters didn't give similes recklessly. Each simile must be accepted only from the particular point that it is expected to illustrate. In any case, all similes can themselves only be objectifications. The whole purpose of an analogy is to turn the split-mind from objectifying and thus to return it to its true wholeness. If this is not firmly kept in mind, the purpose of the analogy would be defeated. Thus the classic analogy of the clay and the pot created out of the clay (the pot is only clay given a particular shape) is basically imperfect because it means representing, through objective images, that which is formless!

Similarly, a discussion about whether any object, including the human body, is solid or not is really begging the question, because there is in fact no object but only an appearance in consciousness, and discussing a particular quality (or the absence of it) in an object could quite easily defeat the purpose because of the implication that there exists an object as such.

True perceiving means perceiving the illusoriness of the pseudo-subject, the sole factor which prevents our BEING that subjective unicity. The moment this true perceiving, this understanding becomes spontaneous, we would be experiencing the Teaching, because then, in the words of the great Chinese sage Shen-hui, we would be having "silent identification with non- being".

Could you sum it up in one sentence?

How about, "true perceiving is a noumenal function in which there is no thing to perceive and no thing that perceives"?

Who am I to argue?!

CHAPTER 13

• *THE ESSENCE OF UNDERSTANDING*

Am I right in thinking that an essential part of the Teaching is that everything that we can perceive and cognize can have no existence other than what appears to exist in "mind", which itself is the content of consciousness?
Well, what are you waiting for?

I thought you were going to draw some conclusions from what you said, which is obviously correct.

I had hoped that in your own inimitable way, you would take up my point and take off on an exploratory trip over the intricacies of truth.

No need for flattery. It did strike me that your opening statement had a rather obvious corollary, but I was hoping it would be you who would undertake the exploratory trip. And incidentally, truth is perhaps the most obvious thing one could find - or not find- and any intricacies in the understanding of it would undoubtedly be of our own making through our incorrigible habit of conceptualizing. If we but stopped conceptualizing, truth would be staring us in the face.

I can see that that makes sense. But what was this obvious corollary to which you referred?

If it is apperceived that whatever is perceived is only an appearance in consciousness (mind), then that apperception must comport the apperception that consciousness cannot have any independent existence either.

Why is that?

For the simple reason that mind-consciousness merely symbolizes what we ourselves ARE; we (as the perceivING) cannot see it as an object, independent of that which is perceiving. The eye can see something else but cannot see itself (without a mirror); the tongue can taste something but cannot taste itself; the dagger can stab something but cannot stab itself.

You mean "we" are consciousness, *and* the supposed "mind". But then why are objects, as appearances in consciousness, created at all?

If you mean *why* do "we" (as consciousness) create objects at all, the answer is that "we" are playing a game, *lila*, wherein the various objects with *nama-rupa* (name and form) come into mutual relationship. If you mean *how* do "we" create the objects - the mechanism - the answer is that objects are created when thinking or conceptualizing goes on, on the basis of the "me" against the "other". The "me" includes friends in a friendly "circle", which expands and contracts, and alters its shape according to the changing circumstances. The "other" refer to the foes in the rest of the world!

In other words, *conceptualizing* turns the mind *outward* and the mind then divides itself into a duality of subject/object and creates objects.

What this actually means is that consciousness - mind, which is "I" (which as noumenon is all I can *be*) creates, *as an apparent object*, something other than I, so that the mind is thus split into me-subject and you-object, "self" and "other". But the significant factor in this mechanism, that is often lost sight of, is the fact that in spite of the division of the mind into me-subject and you-object, *"I" as the noumenal subject always remains as "I"*, devoid of all objective existence and attributes. The *lila* comes into being because each sentient object regards itself as the "me-subject" and the others as the "you-object". Thus "we" are all apparent objects of what we really ARE - "I" noumenon. This situation can be conceived as one single source of light reflected in "ten thousand" mirrors providing infinite variety according to the formation of each mirror and its respective placement.

So the process of objectifying necessitates the splitting of the "mind" notionally (consciousness as "I" remains eternally whole) into relative duality of contrasting elements of subject/object.

The contrasting elements are not merely subject/object which are the basic pair, but all the variable pairs of interrelated opposing concepts like positive and negative, pleasure and pain, love and hate. This is the motivation, the search for pleasure and "love" to the *exclusion* of the interrelated opposites, which is the cause of the supposed bondage.

But what is it that prevents all the "me-subjects" from realizing their true nature as "I"?

What is the medium without which the appearances in consciousness that we are would not be perceivable and cognizable? In order to be perceivable and cognizable, these images have to have "volume", and this volume (form or *rupa*), extended in "space" must have a minimum duration (which we call "time") in which it may become perceivable and cognizable.

This seems fairly elementary.

The truth is very much elementary - basic and simple and rather obvious. It is precisely for this reason that it is overlooked. Anyway, it is, as you said, elementary that the space-time element is merely a conceptual medium in which objects can appear. But it is not realized that this space-time element is obviously not something objective to ourselves as phenomenal objects. Space-time is nothing independent to which we are "bound" but only a sort of mechanical extension that renders us objectively perceptible to subjective perceiving. It is needless to add that *since we are all objects, the perceiving must necessarily be in the totally different dimension of subjectivity.*

I am sorry but I still don't see the point.

Our notion of being in bondage - and therefore needing liberation - is just this very illusion that we are independent entities subjected to duration or time or temporality. It is this apparent temporality which enables the notion of an independent entity not only to exist but to *endure*. If the supposed "me"s did not appear to last - if they were not temporal - would they not be intemporal, which is what I AM, intemporality, whoever says it?

What we have been told by Nisargadatta Maharaj - and other Masters - is that liberation exists in the demolition of the illusion of an independent "me". Has anything been said about duration or temporality?

Do you not remember the advice repeatedly given by Maharaj, that mere hearing by the ears is not enough, that there must be listening by the mind and the heart? And the repeated complaints from people that they seem to comprehend the Teaching at some point of time but they lose it "thereafter". The point is that even if we could remove the notion of "me" for a moment and we do this quite often - its enduring in time remains, and it comes back again and again. We cannot destroy our "me"-ness without destroying its duration - the two concepts are inseparable, two aspects of the same notion.

The logical question that follows is: how do we do that? How do we remove the "me" concept and its duration altogether?

That is just it. In what we are discussing, logic and dialectics do not fare so well because they find themselves out of their depth. Also I am reminded of Maharaj's usual query: Who is asking the question? Who is to "do" anything? The only problem is to apperceive that "time" is not only not something objective to "ourselves" but can only be an intrinsic element of what we appear to be as phenomenal objects in consciousness - mind. There is no need to make any effort to recover our intemporality which we, as "I", have never lost. What is to be apperceived is the basic and fundamental fact that space-time is a mere concept that enables phenomenal manifestation to take place, and that as "I" - which is all that we could all possibly be - we ARE infinity and intemporality. Apperceiving this is experiencing the Teaching. "We" can only experience what we are as "I", and the fact that "we" seem to experience the contrasting elements like pleasure and pain is the ineluctable effect of duality, of which the concept "we" is an intrinsic part. We can truly experience only what we ARE as "I" - there is absolutely nothing else to be experienced. And the understanding, the apperceiving, is itself the doing, the experiencing.

In other words, escape from the subjugation of relative duality consists in identifying ourselves with it, by apperceiving that it is what we are subjectively.

Quite so. With the recognition of temporality as being not external to ourselves, we also realize that temporality and intemporality are inseparable as the twin aspects of what we are - the one appearing in movement and the other static. This is what Nisargadatta Maharaj wanted us to realize when he said "I am time". We all are. We are intemporal as "time" (or duration) and we are time as "intemporality".

CHAPTER 14

• *IDENTIFICATION AND DISIDENTIFICATION*

Nisargadatta Maharaj used to refer to the manifested universe as the child of a barren woman because the entire manifestation was a concept, an illusion. If this is clearly perceived, there should be no question of "bondage".

Quite correct. But by whom will this be perceived? Is this to be perceived by the conceptual subject that regards what it is as an object? If so, it means that one phenomenon as the conceptual subject regards the rest of the universe as an illusion - it excludes itself from the totality of this illusion! What is necessary is the total abolition of any kind of entitification whatever.

Do you mean by that the disidentification of an existing identification?

Not exactly. While the term "disidentification" certainly conveys more appropriately and more accurately what is inferred by the term "enlightenment" or "awakening", it is really not satisfactory inasmuch as "disidentification" presupposes "identification" of one objective entity with another, apart from the implied possibility of "re-identification" with a third object. And this is incompatible with the idea of the annihilation of entitification as such.

The basic element in the phenomenal condition called "bondage" is the functioning of the split-mind in the context of space-time. In it, everything that the conceptual subject perceives, *including "itself"*, appears like an object that other phenomenal objects cognize by its name and form (*nama-*

rupa) and which is also perceptible (at least partially) to "it-self" and that which it regards as "itself". This is the supposed "identification". The apprehension that this is not so, the understanding that "perceiving", like all forms of sentience, is in fact a space-time objectivization of the indivisible condition of "being conscious" (consciousness), of what Maharaj called "knowingness" (*janatepan*) is the supposed "disidentification". Maharaj often expressed wonderment that this truly simple fact should be so difficult to apperceive because of the profound conditioning of *maya*.

"*Maya*" being the multiplication of objects through the splitting of the mind into subject/object?

Correct. This basic error can be rectified by the apprehension that the multiplication of objects does not *necessarily* imply division of consciousness. Duality is merely the medium through which manifestation takes place. "Dualism" which creates the "me" and the "other" is a corruption of duality. In other words, apparent subjectivity is somewhat like one's image reflected in a number of mirrors, varied in reception according to the form, quality and situation of each mirror. Thus seen, the entitification of phenomenal subject disappears and the subject, even regarded as singular, is apperceived as noumenon and everything sensorially perceptible is apperceived as phenomena. *No subjective element remains phenomenally at all*. This apperceiving means experiencing the Teaching.

Is that all there is to it?

"We" can, for all practical purposes, assume that this is all there is to it.

I sense impending trouble!

Not really. All I would add is the fact that all that is said - here or anywhere, now or at any time - can only be conceptual. What is referred to as consciousness or the whole-mind or sentience is only a concept but it is immensely helpful as a symbol for what we ARE. What we ARE, we can only BE - and then there would be no need for any "pointing" by anybody for anybody. Being without the slightest touch of objectivity, what it is can only truly be apperceived as "I", always the subject of all objects cognized.

Perhaps that explains to a certain extent what Nisargadatta Maharaj meant when he said, "I must be present before anything can happen".

In this instance as in others, a certain amount of misunderstanding used to arise in spite of the repeated reminders from Maharaj that the listeners must not listen to him as one individual entity to another. Obviously Maharaj meant the subjective, noumenal "I", whereas most listeners would understand Maharaj's "I" to mean the "me" that they have in mind when they themselves use the first person singular. Identification occurs when the "I" becomes an object which is identified with a phenomenon: nominative "I" becomes the accusative "me", with the false dialectical process.

Dialectically, "I" must necessarily always be a singular that cannot in any circumstances have plurality. The accusative of "I" can never be "me" because that would not only be self contradictory but meaningless. As subject there can only be "I", whoever says it: as subject "you" is always I; as an object I am always "you". That the objective personification of the subjective "I" has not taken place in the child (because conditioning has not yet taken place), is seen when the child almost always says "Ravi is hungry", *not* "I am hungry". "I" can only be subject in all circumstances. The point in Maharaj's statement "I must be there, whatever happens" should now be clear. Whatever "happens" is in phenomenality in which "I" is immanent, but there is no "I" to "do" anything. It is in this sense too that Maharaj used to say "I am not, but the apparent universe is my self".

Does this mean that nothing can appear to be done?

On the contrary, the apparent universe depends entirely on "action". But such action cannot be attributed to any act-*er*.

It is in fact an apparent functioning which we know as our "living", a functioning that occurs, as movement in consciousness, in a media known as space-time.

In other words, all functioning is in spite of us, not because of us?

As Maharaj has said some time or another, it is always I that see, but cannot see my seeing; it is always I that hear, but cannot hear my hearing; I taste but cannot taste my tasting; I smell but cannot smell my smelling; I touch but cannot feel my touching. Nor can I cognize any cognizing of any part of this functioning.

You mean everything happens only in consciousness, only in my mind as the apparent perceiver?

"Your" mind is only apparently yours. It is not "yours" as such but what you *are*. If you become conscious of something, then you become the subject and that something becomes the object. The basis of consciousness being duality, this subject/object relationship becomes a perpetual regression in duality, which can stop only when duality ends in unicity. It is for this reason that what-you-are, and what-I-am, as pure subjectivity, cannot be aware. We can only *be* awareness, not aware of the awareness.

CHAPTER 15

• *THE PERPETUAL PROBLEM*

In the silence of the mind, when the mind is quiet, the first stirring gives rise to the persistent question: what does all this manifestation, in which we all mutually appear, mean? And where does it spring from?

The persistence is due to the fact that consciousness, which has fallaciously identified itself with the individual psychosomatic apparatus as the "me", is constantly seeking its own source. And the joke, as Nisargadatta Maharaj used to say, is that all there is, is consciousness; therefore, what consciousness is seeking as its source is itself! The search goes on until there is apperception that consciousness is the "I" awareness that cannot be aware of itself because awareness knows no self of which it could be aware. Divided and split into cognizing subject/cognized objects, I cognizes every conceptual thing that can be cognized except that which is cognizing. That which is cognizing is not conceivable since it is no thing; and it is no thing since it is not conceivable!

This is so simple, is that all there is?

It is simple when there is apperception - apperception that that which I am (which is all that we are) is the "source-inconceivable", sheer inconceivability, the inability to conceive what I am, not merely the interconnected opposites "conceiving" and "non- conceiving" - the inconceivability which should reveal that the sought is the seeker and the seeking itself.

In view of the inconceivability, how can there be any understanding?

How can "I" be known? I cannot. How can "I" be experienced? I cannot. Only "God", only "*Guru*", can be experienced. Why?Because He is my concept, my object. But, when conceptualizing is in abeyance - the mind is fasting - and time and space are also in abeyance together with all concepts, I AM all that you are as my "self"; how can I have any other?

When the shadow of the ultimate object has disappeared, leaving nothing sensorially perceptible to be found, what then remains is what I am (and what you are). When space-time is in abeyance, and the entire phenomenal universe has ceased to appear, all that remains is the Ground, the Substance, the Source, That which was perceiving the vanished universe when space-time was conceptually present - the conceptual object of the persistent conceptual search: the noumenal "I", pure subjectivity, Awareness not aware of awareness.

I found that the earlier talk we had was on a rather abstract level. Perhaps we could continue that talk in more concrete terms.

The whole problem is that the total phenomenal universe is an appearance in consciousness, without any independent substance to separate it from consciousness. And consciousness, in which "we" all mutually appear as part of that apparent universe (and at the same time perceive and cognize the universe as such) is what we ARE, and *all* that we are. Add to this the fact that consciousness - here and now - is not anything in itself. To objectivize it and make an image of it in the mind (which is just the content of consciousness) would in effect mean making an image of that which is itself making the image of the apparent phenomenal universe (of which we ourselves are a part). Do you not see the absurdity of the whole thing - an absurdity which would render its apprehension forever impossible? It is in this sense

that Nisargadatta Maharaj would sometimes say that understanding of that is impossible: how can you understand
That which is itself UNDERSTANDING - That which we ARE?

What then do we do? How do we proceed?

The understanding of this position itself leaves the way
open for the solution, if it can be called that at all. The whole
point is that "we" are not different from "consciousness"
and therefore we cannot "prehend" it; also "we" cannot be
"integrated" into it because we have never been disinte-
grated from it. Briefly then, as long as the problem is viewed
in relative terms, we can never understand what consciousness is.

Don't you see the obvious answer? It is staring you right
in the face - or perhaps one should say, it was staring you in
the face that you had before you were born!

**I wish you wouldn't talk in riddles. As far as I can see,
all you have done is point to the impasse. There's a stalemate inherent in the problem.**

That's just it. The stalemate inherent in the problem
shows that the problem has been misconceived. The apprehension of the problem itself provides the answer. When we
are what we ARE - and have eternally been - do we need to
ask what we are? Do we need to be told what that is? Do we
need to name it or describe it? Does light need to know what
it is? Does electricity need to know what it is? If you were
the only human being in the world, would there by any need
for you to know that you were a "human being"? The problem is asked in a mind that is split into subject/object. When
we want to understand, we as subject want to understand
something as an object. How can the split-mind know the
whole mind? Does this not explain why Maharaj repeatedly
said, "understand-ING is all. JUST BE. "?

CHAPTER 16

• *REVERSING INTO THE FUTURE*

I meant to ask you but never got round to it. I have a distinct feeling that Nisargadatta Maharaj once or twice said that many of our problems would never arise if we "reversed into the future".

You are quite right. He did say it and that statement was one of those which seemed to have an almost physical effect on me, of being stunned.

Was it a statement which Maharaj could have made merely in order to impress on his listeners something he had said earlier, or did it have a separate significance altogether? I know he sometimes used the English word "reverse" in his talks.

Quite right. He often used "reverse" in the sense of looking back into time, into the past, for instance when he said, "Reverse. What were you a hundred years ago?" But in this instance he used the word deliberately - he was particular about the words he used, Marathi words of course - to mean that we should reverse or walk backwards into the future. He noticed the powerful impact of that sentence on me, and without a break in the flow of his words, he made me a questioning gesture with his hand. I made an answering gesture of a *namaskar*, joining my palms together and bending my head in respectful gratitude.

What did the phrase signify? I was almost certain I had got it wrong.

What he did was to point out with one powerful phrase the utter futility of what we consider as our volitional actions. We think in terms of doing something or refraining from doing something with the intention that a subsequent event may or may not occur. This view is based on the misconception that the future depends on our volitional actions today. It is this false premise of autonomy and the retribution or reward, which are the basis of volitional ethics, that make for the chains of our supposed bondage.

Did Maharaj then imply that we should maintain a fatalistic attitude towards the future?

Maharaj's counterquestion would have been: "who" is asking the question, and who is this "we" that seems to be concerned? Can we as mere phenomenal objects, appearances in consciousness, have any attitude, whether purposeful or fatalistic? If we looked, without judgement or prejudice, at the panorama of events in the past, would we not come to the inescapable conclusion that the events had a distinct ineluctability about them? Would we not come to the inevitable conclusion that the volition we thought at the time to have exercised was a misconception which only brought about a false sense of achievement or a false feeling of frustration, depending on whether the events turned out to be "acceptable" or not? This is what Maharaj meant by reversing into the future, whereby the looking in the wrong direction would be abandoned, and looking into the future would not be seen fatalistically but with confidence regarding whatever the future might bring. Noumenally, what we were a hundred years ago - and which we ARE and have always been - would be totally unconcerned with past or future. Phenomenally, the understanding of the true position would substantially reduce the fear or anxiety concerning the future events, and *bring about* an attitude of cooperating with and bringing ourselves in accord with what the future might bring.

What you say seems so abundantly clear and logical. Why do we find it so difficult to envisage this?

The reason simply is that our way of thinking has become habitual. Giving up the wrong direction of looking - a sudden jolt by Maharaj was a great help - breaks down the conditioned thinking that creates the supposed bondage. Reversing into the future makes us give up conceptualizing and clearly apperceive that from the viewpoint of the illusory individual, problems will never cease but, from the viewpoint of the totality of functioning that we are, problems can never arise.

What precisely do you mean by the wrong direction of looking?

Look at it this way. If we have placed a bet and we lose, according to our habitual way of looking we would consider that we lost the money *because* we placed a bet. We do not even consider the possibility of the viewpoint that the placing of the bet and the result - either winning or losing - could be one single event so that it could well be considered that the bet was placed only because there had to be winning or losing. It is common experience that one makes an investment on the spur of the moment, for whatever reason, when one had really no prior "intention" of doing so. Our reaction to the result of the investment is one of gratification in our "judgement" if it is fruitful, and of frustration if otherwise. But it would not ordinarily strike us that seeing the investment as the cause, and the profit or loss as the result, is a wrong way of looking at what is one connected event. Our habitual way of looking is based on the illusory concept of volition that seems to compel us to break up an event into cause and effect.

Could you really apply this principle to life in general?

Why not? Have you ever considered why living things eat and reproduce? How much "volition" is concerned in either? Living things eat and reproduce so that living may go on. If you did not eat, you would starve and die, and the animating element would disappear from the body. So, is living the reason for the eating and the reproduction, or is it vice versa - or is it really one functioning in Totality? Which comes first - the living or the eating and the reproducing, the egg or the chicken, the acorn or the oak? And which is the cause and which the effect? No problems would arise if we would but see things as the totality of manifestation, and events as the totality of functioning. The past-present-future is merely the conceptual duration in which the functioning as a whole can take place - as living, as *lila*.

Would this principle which refers to "living" also apply to dying?

Would it not? Think it out for yourself.

You mean, if we lived into the future with a sense of serenity by putting down the ghost of the past, our dying like our living would be infinitely more serene.

Then, instead of believing that our past indicates that we act in a particular way so that our future would turn out the way we want it to, we shall believe that we would act in a particular way so that everything may turn out as it is due to be.

Would not this also presuppose volition?

Volition would then be absent inasmuch as what would be present would be humility (as the absence of anyone to be proud) and relinquishment or resignation (as the absence of anyone to renounce).

Expressed otherwise, you mean that "time" should be seen not as having an objective existence, but merely as an aspect of WHAT-WE-ARE. .

Indeed so. Temporality and intemporality are twin aspects of WHAT-WE-ARE - temporality making possible all phenomenal action while, noumenally, intemporality remains static and eternal.

CHAPTER 17

•   *I AM THE PAIN*

When Nisargadatta Maharaj was suffering from cancer, he said several times that he *was* the cancer. What was the significance of that statement?

The difficulty would not arise if you remembered that Maharaj almost always spoke from his noumenal identity. What he meant was that what we suffer as an experience - whatever experience, "good" or "bad" - is not something external to our "selves", suffered by a "me", but is itself what we who are suffering the experience ARE.

Would you elaborate?

Maharaj repeatedly advised his listeners to make a habit of thinking from the viewpoint ofKrishna and not Arjuna, which meant seeing from "within", from the point of view of what-we-are (not what-we-think-we-are), from the viewpoint of Totality (not that of an individual). Thus perceived, the situation is that, in order to manifest as sentience, "I" must produce the appearance of "space" and "duration" in which to extend Myself conceptually. In this, My space-time universe, "I" appear divided as subject and object in order that I-subject - may experience *as object*. Subject/object relation discriminates sentience in duality by such interdependent opposites as "pleasant and unpleasant", "pleasure and pain". When My subject/object are mutually negated, what remains is I, because sentience is what subject/object is as "I".

I still don't get it.

In brief, what Maharaj meant was that it is identification with *that* object which suffers experience (of cancer), which constitutes bondage, whereas he himself, being THIS experience, is thus devoid of entity and therefore not bound.

You mean suffering is experiencing in the context of duration - in relative duality - and is therefore only a concept?

That experienc*ing* (sentience) is what we are as extended in space-time whilst what we think we are is some "thing", an individual "self", that possesses a body, has sentience, and suffers experience. We must therefore not be identified with the objective medium whereby we are experienced.

But the physical pain!

Pain as an experience relates only to the object and it is consciousness, as sentience, which makes experiencing possible. Reducing pain means sentience being held in abeyance, by whatever available means - deep sleep, sedatives, or *hatha-yoga* - but the fact remains that it is the object, the psychosomatic apparatus, that suffers the experience known as pain. When pain reaches a certain point of tolerance, the apparatus must express the pain, but this limit of tolerance would vary from object to object. Where there is understanding, there would be no identification either with the pain itself or the visible expression of it. It is not that the sage is immune to pain, but it is possible that the limit of tolerance would be extended to a certain extent because of the disidentification. But beyond that point the body would certainly suffer the pain and express it vocally. The point, however, is that the sage would not be identified with the body, and therefore, even if the body cries out in pain, such expression of the pain would be witnessed just like that of any other body. The tolerance of pain would depend more on the natural constitution of the body than on the understanding of one's true nature, and would therefore not be an indication of the "level" of enlightenment!

There is also the point that physical pain would comprise a comparatively small percentage of suffering as the word is ordinarily used.

Quite correct. "Suffering" is usually connected with psychic suffering and bondage in metaphysical terms and its experience. What is called "experiencing" is in fact the effect of reacting and has no existence as such. It is the sensual interpretation of the reaction as pleasant or unpleasant, but the point is that it is only conceptual and never factual. Whenever there is experience - cognizance - the presence of a "me" is necessarily there; and vice versa - whenever the presence of "me" is felt, there is invariably an experience. Therefore, there cannot be experience without "me" and no "me" without the experience: they are inseparable.

In the ultimate analysis, since experience is a reaction to stimulus, who is it that reacts?

The direct answer is that who or what reacts can only be the experiencing of the experience, which is "me". When anyone says "I suffer an experience", it is nonsense because the nominative "I" is pure subjectivity and an experience can only appear to be suffered by an objective "me", the two being inseparable. And, it is mistaken identification of "I" with "me", of subjectivity with objectivity, which is the original sin, the "bondage". When we say "I" in relation to the experience, we mean "me", a sensorial mechanism through which experience is suffered psychosomatically.

What this comes to is that "I" experience as "me" through or by means of the sensorial apparatus.

And, it should therefore follow that "I", objectified as "me" - the manifold "me" - am experience as such ("I AM the pain"); and that experience is an interpretation of a sensorial reaction to stimulus, that may be apprehended as the essential manifestation of WHAT-I-AM objectified as "me". In sum, experience is the objective functioning of what I AM. What this truly means, then, is that *living* itself is the experiencing by the manifold "me" as the objective functioning of what I AM. What I AM cannot be phenomenally perceived (except as the manifold "me") because then subjectivity would have to become an object which would then have to have a subject, and so on ad infinitum.

CHAPTER 18

• *VOLITIONAL EFFORT*

Good afternoon. What are you doing, sitting here all alone? Not thinking, I hope! - and I'd guess you're not day-dreaming since you don't have the vacant look of the day-dreamer.

No, I have not been either thinking or day-dreaming. What I have been doing is watching that three month old infant making such strenuous and intense efforts to turn over on its back. It strikes me that the infant is not "aware" of those efforts being made, much less does he "think" that those efforts are being made by him personally as an individual.

That is rather obvious - I would not call it a particularly profound thought!

On the contrary, I feel, if I may say so, that it is indeed a profound observation. Consider the fact that that infant started as a mere sperm cell battling against thousands of other cells to fructify itself and finally succeeded in its efforts. Is it not a humbling thought that one cell gradually developed itself in the mother's womb, collecting various "ingredients" until at the end of nine months it could emerge itself into this world as a new individual appearance. Who made all the necessary effort? And who is making that effort now to turn over on his back? Who told him to do so? Also, is the infant deliberately making efforts to achieve or attain anything?

It strikes me this same infant after a few years, with the dawn of intellect, will begin to think of himself as a separate autonomous entity who has to make personal efforts to attain or achieve personal ambitions and goals.

Right. It is an interesting situation. But perhaps the more intriguing aspect of the matter is what is meant by effort. When Nisargadatta Maharaj declared that "understanding is all", what did he mean? So far as the average listener was concerned, he felt that Maharaj was leading him up the garden path, making a fool of him. This was because all the conditioning over a long period of time had dinned it into him that he should have an ambition and a goal for which he should strive with all his might. And here was Maharaj declaring that all he had to do was to understand; presumably meaning that no further effort was necessary.

Well was that not precisely what Maharaj did mean?

This is what I meant by the intriguing aspect of the matter. We can see that great efforts are being made by the infant to turn over. There is also the goal - to turn over on his back. The point is: who decided on the goal and who is making efforts to achieve that goal? Did that sperm cell make the tremendous effort in order to survive and fructify itself as the goal? Who made the efforts to grow within the womb, and thereafter? Has it not all happened without *conscious* effort, without *volitional* aims and ambitions? Indeed, would you call all this non-volitional activity "efforts"? If so, whose efforts?

What you mean then is that when Maharaj declared that "understanding is all", he meant that no *volitional* efforts, either to do anything or not to do anything, would be necessary.

And that such action would necessarily happen by itself as the natural consequence of that understanding, and that such action, because of the absence of any volition, could be called non-action.

Like the activity of the infant to grow, arising out of the intuitional understanding or knowledge.

Right. It is the powerful conditioning, which has equated all activity with personal volitional effort, that is the cause of all the misunderstanding and misapprehension. The basic point to be kept in mind is that the very manifestation and its functioning is a non-volitional affair (indeed a dream). No part of the activity within that functioning could ever be volitional effort. The very considering of anything as volitional effort is the infamous *karma*. Remembering that, everything remains clear and transparent.

You make it seem simple.

No, that is not so. No one could make anything seem simple (and yet remain the truth) that is not essentially simple. It is only our conditioning that obfuscates what is basically simple.

But the *karmic* idea is the basic principle of a large body of spiritual teaching.

No, that is not correct. It is in fact only an interpretation of the basic principles - an incorrect interpretation. In fact, it is frequently asserted in the *Diamond Sutra* (and elsewhere) that it is contrary to the basic teaching. There is really a simple explanation for this misapprehension. It is a truism that no volitional factor can interfere with the operation of the process of causation. That which is itself the cause of effects - a phenomenal object - cannot introduce a fresh cause (the exercise of volition) in the inexorable chain of causation, because a fresh cause would imply the existence of an independent objective entity. The individual human being is merely an appearance, a puppet.

This subject of *karma* **- and the closely allied subject of reincarnation - is so important that we could discuss it separately in detail. At the moment, the matter of "volition" is fascinating enough.**

In fact "volition" is so fascinating because it is the very base of the question of *karma* and reincarnation. Indeed, without "volition", the other subject would not even arise! Without "volition", *maya* would be exposed in such nakedness that she would have to disappear altogether. To live non-volitionally means to cease to objectify, to cease to interpret on the basis of *nama-rupa* (name and form), to live in freedom, which is what a sage does.

And how does one do it?

That is the most tragic - and the most comic - part of the whole matter! How does "who" do "what"? The most direct answer would be: "By experiencing the Teaching", or, "Understanding is all".

I have certainly fallen into the trap of conceptuality, haven't I?

That is not your special prerogative! Perhaps you might consider who has fallen into what trap? Are not both the "who" and the "trap" nothing more than concepts? You have, as "you", neither any objective existence nor any subjective existence. The difficulty is all a matter of identification and attachment to that identification. In order to renounce attachment, renunciation itself must also be renounced. But, as renunciation itself is an act of volition, what it amounts to is that volition must renounce itself. Volition is only mind, not something we ever "possessed". How can we have anything to possess or to do anything? "We" are only appearances in consciousness. *Impasse?* Not quite. Ceasing to think, ceasing to conceptualize - "sitting quietly", Maharaj used to say, using the word *swastha* (*swa*=self, *stha*=established in) - would bring about whatever is necessary i.e. a vacant or fasting mind in which all problems created by the mind itself would collapse.

All this is not simple is it?

It *is* simple and very clear. All the difficulty and the cloudiness is the handiwork of thought, of intellect. And it is for this reason that Maharaj said "sit quietly" or "JUST BE".

So you're suggesting that we should live non-volitionally. Is that it?

No. That is not it: It is not that I want to be difficult or vexatious, but the fact of the matter is that there can never be a "non-volitional" living as such, for the obvious reason that the very *act* of living non-volitionally would mean volition. In other words, the volition of non-volition! The only way "non-volitional living" can make sense is to let living take place by itself, merely to witness ourselves *being lived*.

As a matter of fact, we are indeed being lived in what the sage Vasishtha asseverates to be the living dream, in which volition cannot possibly have any role to play. The sage makes it very clear (in the *Yogavasishtha*) that life in its seriality is a dream similar in every respect to the personal dream. Volition, therefore, is only an imagined and not actual factor in our lives. Non-volition, therefore means the abandoning of volitional action, not through the apparent volition of the illusory ego that appears to function and "do" things, but as the result or consequence of the understanding itself, the understanding that is the dis-identification with the illusory ego and an identification, *though notional*, with WHAT-WE-ARE. Such understanding, that Maharaj referred to, leaves the mind vacant or fasting so that it can receive the intuitional apprehension which automatically results in the totality of functioning, in which the ego can have no relevance.

Such intuitive understanding - the apperception - resulting in noumenal activity means *experiencing* the Teaching.

CHAPTER 19

• WHAT WE ARE

Why is it so difficult to get a clear idea of what we are, of our real nature? After reading several books on the subject - and meditating on the matter - I get a vague idea but not the conviction I'm looking for. Why is that?

The direct and unequivocal answer to your question would be that what-we-are cannot be comprehended because there is no subject other than what-we-are. In other words, if what-we-are is to be comprehended as an object there would have to be some other subject to comprehend it - and the result of each comprehending subject becoming the comprehended object would be what is called perpetual regression. If you tell a child, in answer to a query, that he was made by God, the query would immediately follow: then who made God?! This progression ad infinitum, of all opposites and all complementaries, is the distinctive feature of the mechanism of duality in which the phenomenal universe appears.

Is that the reason why Nisargadatta Maharaj used to say that it is not possible to *know* what-we-are? We can only BE THAT.

Yes - because knowledge is only the interrelated opposite of ignorance. And what-we-are is prior to both knowledge and ignorance, which can only be concepts. Maharaj also used to define what-we-are as the absence of "presence-and-absence".

I remember that. I was always intrigued by that phraseology, but I know that it has been used by several *Jnanis* to describe the indescribable as simply as possible.

I cannot say definitely but it is my feeling that a young nuclear physicist would grasp it very quickly because he often has to tackle such situations, though of course in a different context altogether. The difficulty of comprehension arises because the whole thing is undoubtedly a concept. And the conceiver of the concept wants the answer to free himself from a conceptual bondage in which he, as a phenomenal object, an appearance, could never possibly be bound. This dilemma becomes doubly confounded because if he says he - the concept - does not exist, the question immediately arises: who says (or knows) that he is not? This is because the statement that "he is not" (or "he does not know what he is") itself clearly implies and demonstrates that the statement is made by that which IS prior to both knowledge and ignorance, and prior to both presence of presence and absence of presence.

So then, it is impossible to comprehend conceptually and dialectically what-we-are.

Perhaps you could put it this way: the not-finding of the answer (to the question "what are we") *is itself the finding*, because if this not-finding leads to the abandoning of the conceptual search and to the apperception of what non-conceptually we are, such abandonment would include not only the search but, far more significantly, the conceptual seeker himself! What the finding would amount to is: *phenomenally* speaking, we can be said to be the concept conceived (the seeker) and that which is conceptualizing (the sought) - the seeker being the sought, and vice versa, in other words, *"conceptuality"*; *noumenally* speaking, we, being "upstream of conceptualization" and thus not able to conceive or be conceived are, in other words, *"nonconceptuality"*.

I must confess that I *feel* the truth of what you are saying but find it difficult to grasp it.

That's just the point! How can you expect to grasp non-conceptuality conceptually? Phenomenally our appearance - what we appear to be - is conceptual, whereas what-we-are, being non-conceptuality itself, is clearly unknowable conceptually, i.e. within the apparent limits of space-time. What-we-are non-conceptually therefore must necessarily be "the not-knowing of knowing", infinite and intemporal, neither any thing nor nothing.

What it means then is that what-we-appear-to-be can never cognize what-we-are because what-we-are is what cognizes.

Right.

CHAPTER 20

• ## *"BONDAGE AND FREEDOM" - SIMPLIFIED*

How far can the concept of "bondage and liberation" be simplified?

Every sentient being is a phenomenon. Indeed, as the etymological meaning conveys precisely, every sentient being - indeed every conceivable thing that is perceived by our senses and interpreted by the mind - is an "appearance" (in consciousness) extended in space and measured in duration, objectified in a world external to that which cognizes it. In other words, that which cognizes it assumes it is the "cognizer", the subject of the object that is cognized, and as such assumes itself as an entity separate from that which is cognized. It is these assumptions that bring about the correlated assumption of bondage. It is simple enough to apprehend that liberation from this assumed bondage is merely the abandoning of these assumptions which are clearly apparent, phenomenal and therefore illusory. An "appearance" is something "that appears or seems to be", not something "that is".

Is this not simple enough? An appearance, an object, assumes itself to be the subject of another appearance as *its* object, forgetting that all appearances are objects and the only subject is the source of all appearances. A clear apprehension of this simple fact is all the remembrance that is needed to remove the forgetting that has brought about the supposed bondage. What the mistaken "subject" considers as the reality cognized by himself as a separate entity, is only an appearance in consciousness - this apprehension is itself the supposed liberation from the supposed bondage. With this readjustment or transformation, neither the subject as an entity nor the object as an entity exists as such - and there is no bondage.

Is that simple enough?

Perhaps too simple. Could that be the reason why such enormous conceptual structures have been erected on such a simple base? To make the matter more impressive?

Perhaps.

Would it be correct to say that in order to get rid of bondage, all that needs to be done is to constantly think of this-which-we-are-not?

On the contrary, what is necessary is *not* to think of this-which-we-are-not. What is necessary is that there be no volition in whatever is done - this is the core of the Teaching. Understanding is all. The understanding of THAT, which is all that we could possibly BE, must act directly without the intervention of any volition. Direct action - direct perception - is upstream of discriminating thought and volition.

You mean no action as such is at all necessary?

Let us understand what we are talking about. Bondage is, specifically, mere identification with a phenomenal object - simply the idea that that-which-we-are is an object (psychic or somatic). Released from this mistaken notion of one's personal objective existence, we are free of the supposed bondage.

Enlightenment or liberation is pure subjectivity; what-we-think-we-are is an appearance. How could the manifestation of an appearance possibly affect its source, irrespective of any action supposedly taken by the appearance? A shadow cannot "act" on its substance. The fact of the matter is that all apparent action - therefore all practice of any kind whatsoever - is noumenal. It is noumenon alone who "acts and practices", and phenomena are "acted upon and practiced". But then the practiser and practiced, separated only notionally as what they are not, have always been unseparated as what they ARE. There is no practicer and nothing to practice - no seeker and nothing to seek. Deep apprehension of this is illumination.

If identification with a phenomenal object is bondage, how does the sage continue to live like an ordinary human being after liberation?

It is not the identification with a phenomenal object as such that automatically means bondage. What is responsible for the bondage is not the phenomenal object for the simple reason that the object has no "ens". The object is not an entity. It is the superimposition thereon of the elaborated notion of an autonomous self with supposed independence of choice and action that is responsible for the effects of the apparent "volition" known as "karma" and "bondage".

As long as there is a pseudo-entity, a "you", apparently doing or not doing anything, nothing has spiritually happened. As long as a phenomenon does or does not do anything with a pseudo-entity in the saddle, it is in "bondage". What matters is not the identification with the phenomenal object as such, but the difference between what you ARE and what you think you are - bondage is identification of the former with the latter. Abandoning of this identification is liberation.

In other words, we need not hesitate to use the personal pronoun "I" as speaking from a phenomenon that *appears* to act or not to act, so long as we are clear that we do not regard that phenomenon as having any independent nature or volition. Then, such phenomenon is not "in the saddle", and the "I" is not identified with it. Then, there is no bondage.

The final stage of fulfillment or deliverance - it can only be conceptual when put into words - is the total integration when "I" and "you", subject and object, lose all significance because of the apperception that phenomena are noumenon, and noumenon is phenomena.

Has what is called seeing phenomenally and seeing noumenally anything to do with bondage and liberation?

It has everything to do with bondage and liberation. Seeing phenomenally means seeing objects from the point of view of the pseudo-subject and involves identification with a phenomenal object as a separate entity with autonomous choice and volition - it means bondage.

Seeing phenomena noumenally is in-seeing or true seeing - in non-objective relation with "things" - which is liberation. Seeing noumenally is seeing phenomena not as *our* objects, as being "without", but subjectively, as being "within". It is reuniting the separated with their integer that we are - reidentification of the dis-united, making the divided mind whole.

Is it possible to put the matter of "bondage" (and liberation) in, say, one sentence?

Yes, certainly.

Well, let's have it.

As long as there is a "me", thinking and feeling as a "me", that "me" is an object and is in bondage. Why? Because all objects are necessarily in bondage.

Would your statement hold true even if that "me" should have succeeded in freeing itself from fear, desire, etc. ?

Even if a "me" has succeeded in freeing its "self" from all kinds of affectivity, it matters little so long as the freed "self" is still there as a "self", considering itself freed and continuing to act as a freed self. The freedom from an apparent incubus (and its oppressive influence) is not really of the essence. What is of the essence is that *the entity needs to be eliminated*, not the affective manifestation (like fear, desire etc.) of the pseudo-entity. It is the presence of the phenomenal pseudo-entity which constitutes bondage, and the absence of which is freedom, liberation from the tyranny of the conceptual entity.

Why should an entity be inescapably bound?

Because an entity is an object that usurps and assumes the subjectivity of the subject of which it is an object, and thus falls into the bondage of apparent causality. It is for this reason that Nisargadatta Maharaj - and other Masters - have unequivocally stated that the presence of a seeker entity inevitably prevents enlightenment - there is no difference between ignorance and enlightenment as long as there is a conceptual entity to experience either condition.

You mean only in noumenality can there be absence of bondage, and therefore there is freedom only in non-objective, noumenal seeing?

Yes, that is it exactly. Only volition-free, noumenal living can be free.

Could you tie it all up in a neat little package?

How about this? Separateness is the essential intrinsic condition on which the conceptual bondage depends, and abandoning of the separateness means freedom from that bondage. The illusion of separateness arises owing to the apparent presence of objects whose cognizer forgets his own objectivity and assumes to be their subject. The real position is that the supposed subject is himself an object like all other appearances in the manifestation, whose cognizer is nothing other than the cognizing itself - the nature of cognition - so that the cognizer and all that is cognized form an innate, inseparable Totality, or whole-mind. Separateness as conceptual subject/object relation exists in the split-mind of duality, and the realization of the essential wholeness demolishes the separateness of any operational center in the psychosomatic apparatus. Such realization is freedom from bondage. It is liberation from solitary confinement in the prison of "self" into the total freedom of universal identity - experiencing the Teaching.

It has been said by many Masters at many times in many ways that bondage is merely bondage to a concept. I have a vague idea of what is meant, but it is certainly not clear.

It is the illusory entitification which is "bondage" and the cause of all the entraining suffering - bondage is bondage to that concept of entitification. The concept, however, must remain nothing but a concept; and factually there never has been, never could there be, any such thing as an entity to be bound. Our happiness, our suffering, our bondage - our "fall" out of paradise from the garden of Eden, or any other metaphor from any religion - is entirely the effect of the identification of what-we-are with the cognizer element of the pseudo-subject in the duality of our split mind. Such entitification brings into an illusory existence the concept of a supposedly autonomous individual able to exercise personal volition according to his own sweet will and pleasure.

The fact of the matter is that what-we-are (noumenon or whole mind or universal consciousness), objectively manifested as the totality of phenomena, has no objective existence other than as the Totality so manifested. It is simple to apprehend that what-we-are, having no objective existence as such, cannot possibly be subject to either bondage or liberation. In other words, our bondage (and the allied suffering) can only have a conceptual basis.

I think Maharaj once said that duration or time is the very basis of bondage, that time is itself bondage. I do not remember his elaborating on that statement. Could Maharaj have said it or am I under some misapprehension?

I must compliment you on the attention you obviously gave to Maharaj's talks - at least this particular one! Maharaj certainly must have said it because it is so very true.

We have seen how bondage is essentially bondage to the concept of the entity. It is not possible to conceive of anything other than in the context of time or duration. A concept needs duration like any other movement in consciousness. The apparent bondage of phenomenal identification, of entitification, is entirely an effect of seriality or time. Therefore, freedom is liberation from the bondage of duration. As soon as there is integration into temporality, all concepts of bondage and liberation (and the allied notions of *karma* and "re-birth") all being causal, temporal phenomena dependent on sequence, must instantly vanish into thin air.

The manifestation of the apparent universe in consciousness takes place through the five senses which perceive it and the sixth which cognizes it. Such manifestation composed of the three components of phenomenal measurement (volume, or space) could not have taken place without an additional measurement which is time (duration), in which the manifested events could be cognized. The whole mechanism constitutes the objectivization of what is subjective (non-objective) and formless and intemporal.

You mean the unmanifest intemporality has been made objectively manifest through the medium of the concept of "time".

Quite so. The tri-dimensional volume of phenomena has been made manifest by means of the seriality of "time" as duration. Duration is the essence of all concepts, including that of bondage and liberation, *karma* and re-birth. Liberation, basically is freedom from the conceptual chains of duration and entitification.

CHAPTER 21

•   *SPEAKING OF GOD...*

It seems to be expected, amongst the spiritually sophisticated, to say that God is a concept. I wonder how many have gone into the matter. So I'll ask you: What is God?

What a question! And you should ask that!! How could there possibly be such a thing as God? God is not an object.

God is not an object - so then what?

God is subjectivity - the only subject of all objects - subject of the subject-object that one thinks of as "oneself", mistakenly of course.

How do you mean?

What are you phenomenally? - nothing but an appearance in consciousness. You think you are the subject of all others as objects. But in fact, you and I and every sentient object subjectively, noumenally, could only be whatever noumenon - or Godhead - is.

What exactly do you mean?

I mean that Godhead - and each one of us (not as phenomenal objects) - is the presence of what-we-are, which is the absence of what-we-think-we-are.

And what is that?

Our total objective phenomenal absence, which can be the subjective noumenal PRESENCE OF GOD.

You surely don't mean that objective phenomena disappear!

Of course not. "Our total objective absence" refers to the disappearance not of an objective phenomenon as such, but of the identification with an objective phenomenon that we think we are. In other words, we are not "this" thing (that we think we are) but THAT which cannot be any "thing".

Why do you say that God is not an object?

If God were an object, he would be one of a thousand objective gods, and not Godhead as you presumably mean.

I am not thinking of idols which are the objective gods.

The moment God is conceptualized, God is turned into a god because any concept of God automatically becomes an idol. And make no mistake, an image of a deity or saint, whether in a temple or a church or any other place of worship, is an idol, whether it is regarded as only symbol or anything else. And, all prayers and offerings to an object, symbol or otherwise, material or conceptual, are prayers or offerings to an idol.

This is blasphemy!

I have only said what is obvious. Blasphemy and offence can lie only in the mind in which such a notion has arisen. What then is blasphemy? I shall tell you. Blasphemy is any and every action done otherwise than in the presence of God. This is clearly stated in the *Bhagavad-Gita*. And let it be clear, by the presence of God, I do *not* mean the presence of an object, an idol. Irrespective of the presence or absence of an object, an idol, *what the "presence of God" means is the absence of the presence of the self*. It means the immanent divinity.

What do you mean by the absence of the presence of self?

A self that prays humbly to God, and a self, without any personal identification, that IS God, are essentially the same. Let it be clearly understood that by "humbly" is *not* meant "without pride" because then humility would merely be a counterpart of pride. By "humility" is metaphysically implied the absence of any entity to be either humble or proud.

All this is extremely enlightening, but, do you know, I feel that you have demolished some time-honored. . .

Time honored what? Slogans, *clichès*, soporifics?

Maybe so. But they did and do give one a sense of security.

Do you know what Nisargadatta Maharaj used to say about these symbols of security? I don't think he ever asked anyone to give them up even if the sense of security was really a false one. He merely suggested that one might carry on as before *until they dropped off by themselves*. What he meant to convey was: "Let us at least understand. When the sense of guilt that would arise by deliberately giving them up loses the strength of its conditioning, these symbols of false security would fall off. "

Of course there could be other considerations for continuing such practices.

Certainly. Maharaj himself faithfully carried out *puja* three times a day because his *Guru* asked him to. As he said, they don't do anybody any harm and could do a lot of good for those who were not endowed with sufficient intelligence to pursue the course of self-enquiry.

It seems to me that in this discussion about God, we have ignored certain - yes, time-honored - concepts, for instance, "love". Is it not said that God is love?

You have said it. Love is a concept, and God is love. Therefore God is a concept. And of course, "love" is only the counterpart of "hate". I am not unaware how the word is used in a conventional sense, but an inaccurate word could cause confusion and misunderstanding.

What word would you prefer?

Actually "LOVE", if used not as an expression of separateness based on emotion, but to indicate compassion - *Karuna* - is that which holds the world together in "at-one-ment". Preference, like difference, is purely a phenomenon in duality. I would, however, use the word "unicity", though using any word somehow seems degrading because no word could describe the indescribable and, of course, a word itself is a temporal creation.

So "unicity" it is. God is unicity. It does convey a sense of totality.

Also, let us not forget that "love" is an expression of separateness because you are expected to love "others". In unicity we do not love others - we ARE others; and our phenomenal relation with "them" is non-objective, direct, spontaneous, and immediate.

What about "prayer".

Of course, the prayer. What would you pray for - more rain and better crops, or perhaps increased industrial production? A substantial rise in exports?

Now, let's not be flippant.

Oh, I assure you I am not. What I meant was that the word prayer is generally understood as solicitation, which can be seen by the fact that the word "pray" is generally followed by the word "for". Prayer truly means communion. Indeed, prayer *is* communion, just like meditation is when there is no meditator and nothing meditated upon.

What is it you are trying to say?

Nothing at all - except perhaps that there cannot really be any significance in either praying to (and adoring) a concept of a paternal and merciful deity as "God", or in cursing and loathing a concept of an inimical and merciless one as "the Devil", for the simple reason that there can be nothing for either to be other than what we ourselves ARE, who are doing it.

Then, what would you have me do?

I would not have you do anything, or not do anything. That is the whole point. As Nisargadatta Maharaj said, understanding is all. JUST BE. That would be experiencing the Teaching.

CHAPTER 22

• *OBJECTIVE ABSENCE IS SUBJECTIVE PRESENCE*

I am back to what you would call the "Mahavakya approach". What would you say if you were asked to state the one thing without the profound understanding of which nothing else could be valid.

And with the profound understanding of which everything else would follow naturally?

Exactly

I would say, "the final, the irresuscitable, total absence of oneself". If this is completely comprehended, everything else would naturally follow.

Who is to comprehend this completely, if there is no "oneself?"

Nobody - no body. It is "I" who comprehend it. "I" who do not now exist, never have existed, and never will exist *as oneself*. Apperception that objective absence is subjective PRESENCE means total release.

But you are posing a problem that is insoluble: a self-supposed - and therefore illusory - entity cannot be liberated unless it abolishes itself, and, on the other hand, unless it is liberated it cannot abolish itself!

There is an answer and that is: To a question posed in the form of a vicious circle, in the context of a sequential duration (itself a concept), there can indeed be no answer. Release the problem from the conceptual context of duration, and the problem disappears. In conceptual duration, the supposed experiencer does not have any existence other than as an appearance, and the imagined experience of liberation could be only a temporal illusion and not a factual occurrence, and therefore there can be no release as such. And outside of a time-context, there can be no entity to be abolished and therefore no question of any liberation.

In other words, as you have been saying, from the individual's point of view problems will never cease; from the viewpoint of Totality, problems can never arise.

Quite so. Phenomenality *as such* is not different from noumenality since they are merely two aspects of unicity - one with form and in movement, the other without form and in quietude.

Where then is the basic fault?

The concept itself is the basic fault. The self-supposed illusory entity neither exists nor does not exist. It cannot "either exist or not exist". As Nisargadatta Maharaj used to say, how can anything factually happen to what is merely a phenomenal appearance, the noumenality of which (the substance, the ground) is transcendent to all concepts including the basic conceptual media of space and duration in which phenomena are extended? As Maharaj put it, "all that the illusory entity can be (noumenally) is the *absence of its phenomenal non-existence*".

Again we come to objective absence is subjective presence.

Yes. But the "objective absence" truly means not just the absence of presence-and-absence, but the absence of the "the absence of presence-and-absence" - the absence of that kind of absence which is neither presence nor absence.

A sort of double absence?

The double negative. Indeed that is what Nisargadatta Maharaj implied, and what is precisely so described by Taoist Masters like Shen Hui. That is also discussed in some detail by Saint Jnaneshwar in his *Amrutanubhava*.

Could we discuss this a little further in more detail? Perhaps it is important.

Indeed it is most important. Everything in phenomenality is a concept. The double negative, intended to get rid of duality irrevocably, must therefore also be a concept; but it is like a thorn that is used to get rid of a thorn imbedded in the foot and then is thrown away along with the imbedded thorn. The double negative exposes the inexistence of the supposed entity even beyond both existence and non-existence. Thus, there are self-contradictory opposite concepts like non-being and being, non- manifestation and manifestation, the former being negative, the latter counterparts being positive. It is important to note that their assimilation results not in the union of the two concepts (because it is psychologically impossible for two thoughts to be united) but in their negation. They abolish each other into a third concept of voidness, which is the wholeness resulting from such negation.

But where does the double negative come in?

The double negative comes in because the negation of the two conceptual positive and negative counterparts still leaves with us its ghost in the form of a third concept keeping us bound - that of voidness. Thus, when objective presence and objective absence as such are superimposed, there is no longer either presence or absence, for each counteracts and annihilates the other. But then there is the resultant absence, and *the conceiver of that absence*! He cannot even say "I am not", for in saying so he demonstrates that he is. What the double negative does is to *negate the resultant absence*.

This further negation is the absence of that kind of absence which is the absence of presence. In other words, the essential negation is that of whatever is conceptualizing these absences.

Could you put it in some other way?

That wouldn't help. What needs to happen is instant apperception.

Even so, take a crack at it.

Well, we could state the totality of all phenomenal manifestation in three segments that would cover everything and yet be self-evident truths, in the following manner :

a) we abolish opposing positions in space by stating that noumenally there is "neither here nor there";

b) we abolish opposing positions in time by stating that noumenally there is "neither now nor then";

c) we abolish opposing positions of "me" and "not me" (or other) by stating that there is "neither this nor that".

All the three statements between them abolish opposing positions of the thinker in both space and time. But the thinking entity as such remains intact. In other words, while the entity as subject is removed not only from space-time but even from identification with subject-object, *this very removal affirms its existence - who is removed*? There continues to be a "who" who has been removed from space, time and subject-object identification. Thus while their relative positions have been abolished, space-time-thinker all continue to exist as underlying concepts; and until these remaining objects are further negated, their subject - the entity - remains intact. To put this differently, the usual negation formula "neither (exists) nor (does not exist)" is thus inadequate and what is needed is a further negation - the "negation of neither----nor---". To give you a very rough example:

When the TV is "off" there is the absence of pictures onthe screen.

When the TV is "on" there is the absence of absence (of pictures).

When the TV station is shut off, there is the presence of absence.

When the TV tower itself is removed there is the absence of"presence and absence of absence"

How does this double negative become effective?

The double absence or the double negative will mean the abolition of "no-space" (in addition to the first negation of space) and of "no-time" (in addition to the first negation of "time"). And such abolition of "no-space" and "no-time" will mean the abolition of the conceptual beingness of their subject-entity, because, while the absence of space-time is conceivable, the further absence of no-space and no-time is INCONCEIVABLE.

Isn't this a confusing way of expressing the matter?

It is certainly confusing. But the whole point of the matter is to emphasize that while we could, and do, use the word "absence" to the whole negation, we must never forget what the word "absence" encompasses and embraces. If there is a clear apprehension of this fact, then it should be apprehended that the absence means:
a)the absence of neither here nor there
b)the absence of neither now nor then
c)the absence of neither this nor that
and thereby the absence of space-time and of the conceiver of space-time and the absence of "me"(self) and of a conceiver of "me" (self).

It is precisely for this reason that Nisargadatta Maharaj used to call phenomenal manifestation "the child of a barren woman". Whatever concepts you may have and may form about manifestation would be subject to the understanding that you were talking about what is *totally inconceivable*.

How would the double negative work in practice?

The perceiving in depth of the three absences based on the double negative would lead to the apperceiving of our own objective absence, our total absence of "ens". That, in its turn, would lead to our apprehension that we cannot comprehend what-we-are because what-we-are is nothing objective that could be known, and also because there cannot be any comprehender to comprehend what-we-are.

Is there not a flaw in the double negative inasmuch as the double negative may not stop at being "double" and may well become a perpetual regression?

That's a good question. The double negative could be seen as only a "dialectical wheeze" to escape from duality by means of duality. But then, as has been pointed out, it is used as a thorn to uproot another imbedded thorn. Even so, it is not really the concept that matters but the fact that the conceiver of the concept (whatever it may be) continues to remain. And it is he who is at once bound and never could be bound. Nor can he say "I am not" for in so saying he clearly demonstrates that he is! He cannot take shelter behind "immanence" because even the most impersonal immanence would still be an objective concept.

Have we reached an impasse then?

Not really. What the double negative really accomplishes is to draw attention to the fact that the usual simple negation "neither is nor is not" is not adequate enough to demolish the supposed entity. Also, it points to the fact that the absence of the absence of nothing is the clearest indication of what non-conceptually we are - that it is conceptually impossible to know what we are. We are left with no alternative but to abandon the search, which, together with the abandonment of the seeker, itself constitutes "finding". The finding is that the seeker is the sought, the sought is the seeker; and that each, being the conceptual half of THAT which cannot be conceived, is "neither is nor is not. "

Could you give an example or two from ordinary life to illustrate the not-finding itself being the finding?

You know the difficulty in giving examples and illustrations to clarify points concerning non-conceptuality. All such examples would be in conceptual duality, and this point would have to be borne in mind very firmly when making use of them.

Still, two examples could be given. One, certain problems in algebra and geometry would be considered as solved when the conclusion "but this is impossible" is arrived at. That the problem is insoluble is itself the solution. The other example would be that of a car stuck in the sand. Any effort made by putting the car in forward gear makes the tires sink deeper into the pit, and the reverse gear has the same effect. Finally the effort to get the car out by using the gears has to be abandoned.

Would it be correct to imagine that as long as one is employing concepts in split mind, every such concept would be subject to the double negative?

That would be correct. Noumenally, every concept is "neither is nor is not", but as soon as a whole-mind is invoked there is no longer a question of dual counterparts, of a perpetual regression. Thus "total phenomenal absence is total noumenal presence" need not imply anything beyond dual concepts. As soon as the statement is apprehended, objectivizing by split mind (through dual concepts) ceases; functioning returns to the source and whole mind is functioning directly.

Nisargadatta Maharaj used to assure us that the complete apprehension of the initial identity of conceptual opposites - even any one such pair - is itself liberation because "to see one was to see all". The perfect apprehension that "total phenomenal absence is total noumenal presence" should, he said, result in immediate disidentification with the pseudo-subject of pseudo- objects (both being only concepts totally devoid of "ens").

And such disidentification leads to integration?

Integration, or perhaps more accurately re-integration, *occurs*. A rare equilibrium between normally excessive positive factors and normally deficient negative factors is generated in a psyche by intensive negation. Such integration causes certain adjustments to arise in that psyche. What happens then is that the phenomenon, suddenly relieved of the cumbersome weight of the ego, feels a tremendous sense of freedom from the burden of pseudo- responsibilities, the heaviness of which it had not until then realized because it had gradually become a normality. Such a sense of total freedom may find expression in diverse ways depending on the constitution and conditioning of that phenomenon. It may laugh hilariously and dance and want to embrace all phenomenal creation. The sudden sense of freedom not unlike freedom from gravity, may express itself in various ways, but the fact to be remembered is that they are all affective manifestations in temporal pheomenality, although they are apt to be misinterpreted as divine grace or love or whatever. The point is that the rest of the phenomenal events of that particular living dream are *not* likely to be changed drastically and would continue as heretofore, ranging from the sagely and saintly to what might be considered "sinful" according to current norms of morality. Serenity may well replace anxiety however, and all that happens henceforward, whatever it may be, would be seen not only as inevitable but as "right and proper".

Very briefly, the double negative or the double absence could be said to be the absence of an entity to be enlightened or not to be enlightened. What remains after the ultimate object has been negated, is "I", the final affirmation of everything that has been denied. The denial refers firstly to the idea of a phenomenal object being "transformed" as an individual entity from what it appears to be into an "enlightened" one. The more important denial refers to the fact that there truly is no "one" to believe that the belief of personal enlightenment is nonsense!

You have again ended on the note of an impasse.

Only from the viewpoint of temporal duality. Your question obviously is: if there is truly no "one" to believe anything one way or another, how can there be any comprehending? The answer is astonishingly simple. An apperception, deep enough to annihilate the "who", does not need a comprehender. Apprehending - apperceiving - does not depend on identity; it is only knowledge in temporality that is so limited. Indeed it is only when the identity is annihilated that apperception - neither knowledge nor not-knowledge, but the absence of both - *happens* spontaneously and instantaneously.

CHAPTER 23

• ## *UNEXTENDED, YOU ARE HOME*

Nisargadatta Maharaj said "JUST BE". Does that not involve a volitional act by an entity?

That there is no such thing as an entity, only an image in consciousness, was the very basis of what Maharaj said. How could he possibly have meant a volitional act by an individual when he suggested that one should just "be"?

What else could he have meant?

In order to avoid any possible misunderstanding, Maharaj always suggested that the listener should:

(a) read the *Bhagavad-Gita* from Lord Krishna's point of view, and

(b) try to go behind the words that Maharaj uttered.

The point was that the listening should be done with a receptive mind; an aggressively critical mind would erect a barrier between the spoken word and the listened word. In other words, there should be an honesty of intent in listening, so that the attention is not on the apparent contradiction but in the real meaning behind the apparent contradiction.

I am sorry but here there is no question of contradiction. Maharaj clearly said, "JUST BE".

Could he not have meant "do not try to *become* anything"? You will recollect that the words "just be" were usually preceded by the words "understanding is all". And the total answer, "understanding is all - JUST BE" was usually given to the query from the listener, "what precisely is one to do?" In short, what Maharaj clearly indicated was that since there was no entity as such, there was nothing to be done, that understanding was all, and that, therefore, in the absence of any positive action, the supposed individual can "JUST BE".

All right, then. Can I "be" it?

Since you already are "it", and always have been, what is there to "be"?

You mean, TO BE is being it, experiencing the understanding - or apperception?

Precisely. Is it not obvious? Any kind of action would need someone to act.

But surely "being" is also a kind of action?

You would not have asked the question if you were not so habituated to conceptualize all the time. Consciously "being" is a concept, a movement in consciousness, requiring duration in conceptual space-time. I cannot "be" what I am!

I just AM?

Yes if you don't think it, let alone say it.

Do you mean I am "nothing"?

You are neither any "thing" nor no "thing".

I get it. You mean, what I am is just "am-ness"?

Of course not. Any kind of "-ness" is essentially a concept of some "thing" conceptually extended in space and duration.

It is absolutely impossible to get a straight answer from you!

How right you are.

Oh! You mean there cannot be an answer except in relativity - that there cannot be a relative answer to a question that is not relative?

At last! The truth of a concept can be found relatively only in the mutual negation of its relative elements, absolutely. It is in the finding that you are aware of that negating, *which cannot be perceived.*

So where does it leave me?

"You" cannot be, because "you" always, being an object, must be conceptually extended, like "me", in space-time. Only I AM - "I" who may be represented by any object extended in conceptual space-time, which is what relativity is.

How so?

Whatever is relative to the absolute is so because of conceptual spatio-temporal extension contrasted with that of its opposite. Both being mutually interdependent, such mutual extension is abolished by their mutual negation, by their superimposition into a phenomenal void.

Phenomenal void?

Phenomenal void which is the noumenal potential plenum, from which may arise all phenomenality.

In other words, the abolition of the conceptual extension in space-time abolishes relativity, revealing what-we-are, spaceless and timeless. That is all?

That is all. Apprehend extension, and you're home. I AM home.

When not extended, I can "be"?

Unextended in conceptual space-time we cannot "be" - we ARE. I AM.

CHAPTER 24

• THE BEGINNING AND THE END

How does experiencing of the Teaching arise?

Experiencing arises in the culmination of the beginning and the end of the Teaching.

Culmination of the beginning and the end?

What is the essence of the Teaching?

I would say that the essence of the Teaching is that any effort by an entity to improve himself or liberate himself as an entity, would be a waste of time.

Absolutely correct. Is that not the beginning and the end of the Teaching? Did not Maharaj say quite often that there was nothing for him to teach and nothing for the visitor to learn, that they all ARE what he is?

You mean that is the culmination of the beginning and the end of the Teaching, - and that is experiencing?

Maharaj had nothing to teach other than the understanding that there is no entity to be "liberated" or "awakened" or "enlightened" by any Teaching. It is the beginning because unless there is apperception of this fundamental truth, all Teaching, methods and practice are not only a waste of time but only serve to reinforce the illusion of such an entity. And it is also the end because the apperception of that is itself the only enlightenment there could be.

I understand. What then could there be to learn, and who is there to learn? Where is the Teaching and who can there be to teach?

It is for this reason that it is said that the Buddha taught for forty-nine years, and yet no word was spoken. How could he? The Buddha has no mouth - nor any of the other organs or senses, which are the appurtenances of the psychosomatic mechanism. There is only the fundamental understanding, the beginning and the end, the culmination of which is experiencing.

What this amounts to is that we cannot *find* what we are - or *know* what we are because we are already that, and there is no one else who could *find* us or *know* us.

You mean we can never know what we are ?

Don't you see it? All that we can find is that as sentient beings we must always appear as such, objectively extended in the media of space and time. We cannot ever know ourselves as anything but the totality of objectivized phenomena, the existence which is nothing other than conceptual as what is perceived and conceived as appearance. What we are nonphenomenally can never be perceived or conceived because cognizing cannot cognize "that which is cognizing" and we are "that which is cognizing".

You mean that dialectic understanding is not enough to annihilate our misunderstanding?

That is correct. But there is hope. The dialectic understanding of "what-we-must-be" may not be sufficient to break our conditioning, but it could well transpire that the understanding of "what-we-are-not" - anything objective at all - is indeed capable of producing an intensity of conceptual negativity which may annihilate the false identification. There is a solution of continuity between what-we-are and what-we-appear-to-be, like there is between the moon and its image in a puddle. In other words, the intellectual understanding of what we inevitably must be, coupled with the deep conviction of what we are not, could, at some moment predestined in the totality of functioning, bring about the sudden instantaneous enlightenment.

But there has to be an intensity of purpose?

An intensity, yes, but not of purpose. An intensity of purpose presupposes volition on the part of an entity that is wholly illusory. The intensity can only be of the nature of that intensity of attention or concentration which exists when there is total absorption in the doing of an act, when the do-er is utterly absent, when the result of the act is not present in the divided mind, when indeed the divided mind has regained its wholeness.

And the understanding that has thus become unitary or noumenal understanding can never again revert to its earlier division?

That is correct. Then, the understanding of the Teaching becomes the experiencing of the Teaching. The annihilated do-er remains annihilated, and, knowing the source of our phenomenal appearance in space-time to be what we noumenally are, we experience the living-dream to its allotted span in peace. More accurately stated, there is no "we" to experience the living-dream. There is only EXPERIENCING of the living-dream.

Arjuna	One of the Pandava brothers in whose war against their cousins, the Kauravas (which is the subject of the Hindu epic *Mahabharata*), Lord Krishna (God incarnate) becomes *Arjuna's* friend, philosopher, guide and *Guru*. *Krishna* (as the *Guru*) conveys the Supreme Truth to Arjuna (as the disciple) on the battlefield, and their dialogue becomes the famous Hindu Scripture know as *Bhagavad-Gita*
Bhagavad-Gita	(See *Arjuna*)
dhoti	A piece of fine muslin cloth worn by men in India (opposite of *sari*, worn by women)
Diamond Sutra	Perhaps the most famous among the Buddhist *sutras* (a scriptural narrative, a text, traditionally regarded as a discourse of the Buddha)
ens	An entity (as opposed to an attribute); separate existence
guru	Master, enlightened preceptor
hatha-yoga	The physical aspect of the *yoga* system (believed to have been founded by the sage Patanjali) by means of which the individual spirit (*jivatma*) can be joined or united with the universal spirit (*Paramatma*)

janatepan   Marathi word which Nisargadatta Maharaj used as "knowingness", the sense of presence, consciousness

Jnaneshwar   A sage who lived in the 13th century in Maharashtra (west coast state in India), who wrote the *Jnaneshwari,* a tome of a commentary in Marathi, on the famous Hindu scripture known as *Bhagavad-Gita.* He also wrote a small treatise on non-duality, a classic in the field, known as *Amritanubhava* (Experience of Immortality) which is translated into English (with a commentary) -- *Experience Of Immortality* by Ramesh S. Balsekar (Bombay: Chetana, 1984)

jnani   One who has realized the unicity in the phenomenal universe

karma   Volitional action; action for which responsibility is assumed; an event

karuna   Compassion

Krishna   (See *Arjuna*)

lila   The cosmos (the functioning of the Totality) looked upon as the divine play

mahavakaya	The sublime pronouncement. Traditionally, four Upanishadic declarations expressing the highest Vedanta truths: (1) *Prajanam Brahman* (consciousness is Brahman) (2) *Aham Brahmasmi* (I am Brahman) (3) *Tat Twam Asi* (That Thou Art) (4) *Ayam Atrua Brahman* (The Self is Brahman)
Mahayana	One of the two main divisions of Buddhism which moved out of India many centuries ago, and was further developed in China as *Ch'an* and *Zen* in Japan. The other division was known as *Hinayana*.
maya	The illusory appearance of the world; That aspect of Consciousness through which separation gets created: separation between phenomenality (manifest) and noumenality (unmanifest), and separation between one individual and the rest of the manifested world
moksha	Liberation from worldly existence
nama-rupa	Names and forms making up the manifested world
namaskar	Polite or respectful salutation
neti,neti	not this, not this: the analytic process of progressively negating all names and forms *(nama-rupa)* making up the world, in order to arrive at the ultimate Truth

nirvana	Emancipation from matter and reunion with the Supreme Spirit (Brahman)
nisarga	Nature; phenomenality; life
Parabrahman	The Supreme Reality (*Para* - beyond + *Brahman* - ultimate Reality)
prasadic	Given as Grace or by way of blessing
puja	Ritual worship
samsara	Worldly existence
Yogavasishtha	One of the most highly respected works in Indian mysticism, the teaching of the sage Vasishtha imparted to Lord Rama